The Battle of Westport

The Battle of Westport

Missouri's Great Confederate Raid

Paul Kirkman

The History Press

Published by The History Press
Charleston, SC 29403
www.historypress.net

Cover image: *Battle of Byram's Ford*, painting by George Barnett. *Courtesy of the Westport Historical Society.*

First published 2011
Second printing 2011

Manufactured in the United States

ISBN 978.1.60949.006.5

Library of Congress Cataloging-in-Publication Data

Kirkman, Paul.
The Battle of Westport : Missouri's great Confederate raid / Paul Kirkman.
p. cm.
Includes bibliographical references and index.
ISBN 978-1-60949-006-5
1. Westport, Battle of, Kansas City, Mo., 1864. I. Title.
E477.16.K57 2011
977.8'411--dc22
2011002398

Contents

Acknowledgements

The longer I live, the more I realize that the self-made man is a myth. At least in my own life, any successful endeavor I have undertaken has been accomplished with the aid and support of my family, friends and a fair number of strangers, who helped, if not directly, at least indirectly by choosing not to hinder my efforts. This has been especially the case in writing this book. My wife, Shawn, and daughter, Shannon, have both had to adjust to living with the person that I become when engrossed in a new subject. Both of them refrained from the use of violent force to end my rambling explanations of the latest tidbit I'd turned up in a nineteenth-century newspaper or hundred-year-old book. I am thankful for their love, support and restraint.

My editor at The History Press, Douglas W. Bostick, afforded me the opportunity to attempt this subject, with the confidence that my work would be guided by wise and experienced counsel.

My first two opportunities as an author came through my association with the Jackson County Historical Society (Independence, Missouri). Archivist David W. Jackson merits great praise for his tireless efforts on behalf of that organization. I am indebted to Mr. Jackson for the many opportunities to increase and then share my knowledge with others that he has afforded me as editor and coauthor of my previous works. Steve Noll, as director of the Jackson County Historical Society, deserves special mention for allowing me the opportunity to coauthor *Lockdown* with David W. Jackson, in spite of my limited experience. Mr. Noll has, in every instance, aided my advancement as an author and researcher and has been a positive source of encouragement for me. The Jackson County Historical Society is fortunate to have two such dedicated individuals working on its behalf.

The Jackson County Historical Society Archives and Research Library gave me a ready resource for many of the books and documents I used in my research. Photographs from its collection that were made available with permission for this book include jail cells at the 1859 Jail in Independence (gift of Nick Vedros), the Bingham-Waggoner Home (gift of the Bingham-Waggoner Historical Society), the William Bent-Seth Ward Home and Colonel Kersey Coates.

The Westport Historical Society made this book possible in several ways. The most important direct help I received was from the effervescent director, Alana Smith. Mrs. Smith, with a strong sense of what materials would be necessary for this project, enthusiastically and graciously provided direction and help at every step along the way. The paintings and prints she and her husband, Dan Smith, current president of the Monnett Fund, provided from the society's collection, along with research materials from the society's archive, were essential to the successful preparation of this book. The efforts of the members of the society in preserving and collecting, in many cases family papers (as several descendants of Westport pioneers are members of the society), photographs and possessions, have helped ensure that future generations will have access to knowledge of their town. Westport Historical Society, at the Harris-Kearney House, offers a driving tour of the Battle of Westport that includes a stop at the newly formed Battle of Westport Museum in the Main Shelter House at Swope Park (near the Byram's Ford Civil War site). For more information, visit www.battleofwestport.org.

Photographer Jay Rothman of Jay Rothman Writing and Photography is an old college friend of mine who drove across the state from St. Louis to help me out with this project and was able to get some good shots of the Little Blue Battlefield area, showing views from both Price's approach and Moonlight's position on the west side of the river. In addition, he photographed the paintings and other materials from the Westport

Historical Society's collection at the Harris-Kearney House museum. Jay is very meticulous about his work, and I never had any doubts that the materials he produced for this book would turn out great. I appreciate his help and friendship.

The John Wornall House and Museum is poised to take a much larger role in teaching and sharing Kansas City's rich history with its recent merger with the Alexander Majors House museum (and reincorporation as the Wornall-Majors House Museums). Executive Director Kandice Walker, in the midst of this major change, still made time to proffer help and advice, as well as contributing photographs of the portrait of John B. Wornall and the John Wornall Home for use in this book. I am grateful for her help and support.

The Library of Congress website has a wealth of photographs and maps, many of which are in the public domain. Each Library of Congress photograph used in this book has a reproduction number. By entering this number in a search of the website at www.loc.gov/index/html, all the pertinent information for each picture can be found almost immediately. I am grateful for this service made available by the Library of Congress.

Introduction

For most of my life, all I knew about Westport was that it was the "bar district," where everyone went after the St. Patrick's Day parade in Kansas City. I live just east of Kansas City in Independence, Missouri. Independence is my wife's hometown; it's where we met and has become my home. There is a lot of history here. The street I live on used to be lined from end to end with wagons poised to set out on the Santa Fe, California and Oregon Trails. I pass President Harry Truman's home and the Truman Presidential Library and Museum almost daily. Most of the streets and several of the homes in my neighborhood were familiar to Harry Truman. Wild Bill Hickok, Jesse James, Jim Bridger and William Quantrill would have known them as well. I am constantly reminded of the history of my town by the many nineteenth-century homes and buildings that still stand here. Westport and Kansas City were often viewed as different, though, to many Independence residents, as they weren't a part of our hometown. I'm sure some Kansas Citians feel the same way about their older neighbor to the east, Independence. Though the storied past was well represented there, too, the more familiar scenes of my adopted home gained a greater share of my interest and attention.

In 2005, I finished my BA in history (twenty-six years after starting) and was working through an archival internship program with the Jackson County Historical Society. I had written an article for its scholarly *Journal*, volunteered at its museum (the 1859 Jail, Marshal's

Home and Museum) and even submitted proposals for two lectures as part of the State Historical Society of Missouri Speakers' Bureau. I found employment as an archival assistant at the Kansas City Parks & Recreation archives and worked on the lectures in my spare time. The subjects for my programs were the outlaw gangs of Missouri and frontier law enforcement. My research for the lectures ended up providing me with a couple of unexpected opportunities. First, I was accepted as a member of the Speakers' Bureau, where I was able to meet with local history groups from Joplin to St. Joseph. I even was invited to give a presentation at the Jesse James Farm museum in Kearney, Missouri. I met many knowledgeable history enthusiasts and was presented with a variety of opinions and questions about the guerrilla movement's connection to the rise of the outlaw gangs. Second, I was offered the opportunity to expand on my research and coauthor a history of law enforcement in Jackson County, Missouri, with archivist David W. Jackson of the Jackson County Historical Society. *Lockdown: Outlaws, Lawmen and Frontier Justice in Jackson County, Missouri* was the result. It was through the research I did on *Lockdown* that I began to become more familiar with the fascinating history behind General Sterling Price's 1864 raid and the Battle of Westport. When I found out about The History Press's Civil War Sesquicentennial series, I immediately submitted a proposal to write about that great battle, which had passed right down my street more than one hundred years ago, through my hometown and exploded onto the fields south of Kansas City.

The story of the Battle at Westport had been told—and told well—before I came along, and in preparing this book I quickly realized that I was trailing the herd in pursuit of this subject. The Westport Historical Society and the Jackson County Historical Society both had in their archives and within their memberships a great repository of information that was generously made available. The bigger picture was all there but jumbled like pieces of a jigsaw puzzle. It was only with their help putting the pieces together that I was able to see it more clearly. What I hope I have accomplished here is to present the picture in a broader framework. By telling of the place, the people and the long road that led up to the battle, as well as some of the aftermath and long-term consequences, I have tried to bring together a number of resources for the reader that had previously only been available separately. All the pieces I could find have been placed with the intention of making the picture clearer and connecting the various, separate elements of the story. Nearly 150 years have passed since the Battle of Westport, but the drama and tragedy of it all are still compelling. There is courage and sacrifice, love and hate and good and evil aplenty. In short, this is a story worth telling, especially as the sesquicentennial of the Civil War is being commemorated.

The basic framework of what happened at Westport can be found in the reports of the officers of the armies involved. The United States War Department's *The War of the Rebellion: A Compilation of the Official Records of the Union and Confederate Armies* (Washington, D.C.: Government Printing Office, 1880–1901), volume 41, contains most of the related materials. But a sense of the place, people and relative scale of action in the West is essential to understanding the stakes involved in the contest. The Battle of Westport was the largest Civil War land battle west of the Mississippi, and it was fought not early in the war but late, in 1864. Ten years of bloody violence had wracked the Missouri/Kansas border before the first shot was fired at Westport (long before Fort Sumter, for that matter). From John Brown to Jesse James, the characters who peopled the border conflict were larger than life. The battle that took place at Westport was equally as grand. There was finality, an epic quality to the conflict. It drew senators, governors, congressmen (past and future), guerrillas, professional soldiers, raw recruits, unarmed volunteers, state and local militias, Federal troops, civilians and troops from a dozen states. Over thirty thousand men—twenty times the population of the town of Westport—crashed together in the largest and last great battle of the Civil War west of the Mississippi.

The chapters of this book roughly follow my own discovery of the battle's history. Starting with a foundation in the land and people, I tried to get a sense of not only how the area developed but also why. I looked into the people's story, where they came from, why they came, what made them choose to stay and build here. Westport was built a mile from the Kansas territory, perched on the overland trails that led to markets in Mexico and other points west. It had a vested interest in westward expansion, trade with Native American tribes and the produce of the slave economy that had developed in western Missouri.

The conflict over slavery in Kansas and Missouri was played out on the national stage, and Westport was ultimately swept up in the storm it created. The murder and mayhem perpetrated by extremists on both sides of the border fed the hatred and division that would lead to civil war. In a small frontier community like Westport, the elites made up a tight and tiny group; the passions sown by civil strife during the secession crisis in Missouri tore at the core of their connections. The Border War and secession crisis seemed essential to the narrative. The destruction of middle ground and the imposition of martial law changed the dominant culture in the area and made the fight personal. I felt it was more important to understand the feelings and reasons motivating the actors than to try to seriously justify the hellish actions of either side, regardless of the rightness or wrongness of their cause.

The chapters describing Price's raid and the march to Westport were essential to introduce the players and stakes in the contest, and the story of the battle itself merited another chapter as well. The morning after fascinated me even though it covers only part of one day. Only survivors of great calamity can truly comprehend the scope and scale of such a tragic experience. How the people of Westport and the men who had fought there faced a new day is the focus of one chapter. The long retreat and pursuit from Westport punctuated the mistakes and successes of both armies. Price's slow pace and stubborn clinging to his wagon train brought on the folly at Mine Creek. An ever-shrinking pursuit force due to Union turf wars over command, coupled with Shelby's gallant rearguard actions, prevented the Federal pursuit from destroying the remainder of Price's army at Newtonia.

In the final chapter, we peek into the future of Westport and the men who fought in the battle. A substantial number of the leaders in the Battle of Westport became leaders in civilian life as well. Both the famous and infamous seemed to be disproportionately represented among the participants. The sum is a story that bookends the origin and evolution of the town of Westport through the Battle of Westport, Price's Missouri Raid and the postwar lives of the survivors—all tied together in one volume.

The Road to Westport

The road to Westport was paved with good intentions. President Thomas Jefferson had good intentions when he acquired Missouri as part of the Louisiana Purchase. His initial plan of securing the port city of New Orleans from Napoleon led him to a crisis of conscience, as a strict interpretation of the Constitution denied him the power to make such a treaty. Yet it was clearly in the nation's interest to have possession of such a valuable position on the Gulf and at the mouth of the Mississippi. When his representatives returned with a treaty for the purchase of Louisiana Territory, he chose to support it. The measure of the land and its true value was unknown, yet Jefferson saw in it a chance to provide for the young nation's need for future expansion, as well as a hindrance to European aspirations on the continent. Into this vast new frontier went explorers and settlers, but they were followed by the same old politics and quarrels that had given birth to the nation. The principles that led to a fight for freedom for America would lead to a fight for freedom within it. The controversy over expansion of slavery became a central feature of the American political landscape of the first half of the nineteenth century. As territories applied for statehood, efforts to maintain the status quo led to ever-greater polarization. Out of Jefferson's new wilderness would come a change in the balance of political power in America, and the price in both blood and treasure would be much dearer than he could have imagined.

President Thomas Jefferson's Louisiana Purchase extended the borders and the dispute over slavery. *Courtesy of the Library of Congress.*

Pioneers traveled to or through the new territory in Missouri with good intentions. Following the natural course of access to the interior, the three great river systems leading into the state (Ohio, Mississippi and Missouri) served as routes for exploration, transportation and trade. French explorers coming down from Canada or up from New Orleans had long plied these river roads. However, settlement had been a slow process, as many recoiled at the isolation and perils of the frontier, especially those with families. To encourage emigration, the Spanish (who had received control of the area from the French in 1763) had given land grants to many pioneers like the Boone family. Daniel Boone, his sons and their families settled near Defiance, Missouri, about 1799. Like the majority of Missouri's first wave of American settlers, Boone was of Scots-Irish descent and had lived in parts of the South where slavery was common, at one point owning seven slaves himself. The French had introduced slavery to Missouri in their mining operations in the early eighteenth century, but many of the Southerners who had come from Kentucky, Tennessee and Virginia brought slaves with them as well.

The Spanish returned control of Missouri to the French in the Treaty of Ildefonso in 1800, but all the details weren't worked through until 1803, at which time Napoleon quickly sold the area to the United States. The Louisiana Purchase accelerated a settlement pattern that had already started, as American frontiersmen sought and found opportunity in the wilderness. Fur trapping, trade with Native Americans and mining, along with hunting and small-scale farming, were all open to souls brave enough to leave the eastern colonies and enter the West. After the Louisiana Purchase, reminders of the French and Spanish presence in Missouri would remain in place names like Versailles and New Madrid, but most of the communities were quickly engulfed in the wave of American immigration that began with the new century.

The Missouri Compromise of 1820 brought Missouri into the Union as a slave state while counterbalancing its Senate power with the admission of Maine as a free state. Part of the price of the compromise would be that Missouri was singled out to be the last new slave state within the Louisiana Territory north of the Mason-Dixon line (which was extended to include the southern border of the state).

In the thirty years following the Louisiana Purchase, Missouri's non-native American population exploded from around 2,000 in 1803 to 19,000 by 1810, to 66,000 in 1820 and to 140,000 in 1830. The majority of these early settlers came from slaveholding states; however, most of them owned few or no slaves. These were the trappers and frontiersmen, as well as the pioneers and risk takers who would plant many of Missouri's first American communities a few cabins at a time.

The Missouri River and Boone's Lick Trail that roughly paralleled it were conduits that expanded the slave economy into central and western Missouri. Adjusting for different farming conditions, most slave owners along the Missouri replaced cotton as a cash crop with tobacco or hemp.

Native American tribes were continually under pressure to sell or simply vacate their lands by not only settlers but also the United States government.

President Andrew Jackson had good intentions for his constituency in the South (including Kentuckians and Tennesseans who were expanding settlement into Missouri) in promoting the removal of Native Americans from east of the Mississippi River to government lands in the West. As a popularly elected president, his policies expanded the franchise, land ownership and the prosperity and political ascendancy of the Democratic Party of the South. They also extended slavery and forced the removal of thousands of Native Americans from their lands. Eastern tribes like

President Andrew Jackson had thousands of Indians "removed" to Kansas Territory. *Courtesy of the Library of Congress.*

the Delaware and Wyandotte ended up in Kansas Territory, as did the Shawnee, the Kickapoo and many others.

Jackson was not alone in his push for Native American removal. Isaac McCoy (a Baptist missionary to the Shawnee who had removed from Ohio to Kansas Territory) was one of many who legitimized removal as a humanitarian act. He argued that only in isolation from exploitive and corrupting white settlers would the Native Americans be safe long enough to adjust and survive. McCoy even laid out plans to build a great reservation or homeland for all the eastern tribes in the western plains. Following the Shawnee with his family to Kansas Territory, Isaac McCoy built his home on a hill south of the Missouri River (where St. Luke's Hospital on the Country Club Plaza now stands).

In 1829, the Shawnee Indian Mission School was established at Shawnee, Kansas, by Reverend Thomas Johnson under the direction of the Missouri Methodist Conference. Ten years later, the school was moved to its current location, two miles southwest of Westport. The brick buildings there would provide offices for the first territorial governor of Kansas (Andrew Reeder), the meeting of the first territorial legislature was held there and Union forces would camp on the grounds there before the Battle of Westport.

Platted by McCoy's son, John Calvin McCoy, Westport was located in Jackson County, Missouri (one of the earliest of many places that would bear the controversial, yet popular, president's name; it should be noted that Jackson County was named after General Jackson two years before he was elected U.S. president). Trade with the Shawnee and other tribes living nearby was a significant factor in the town's early success.

Archaeological evidence points to settlement of the Hopewell tribe in the Kansas City area as early as AD 300. But in the 1700s, the primary tribe in Missouri (south of the Missouri River) was the Osage. At first, contacts with Spanish and French explorers led to trade. In the 1760s, there was a well-worn trail across what would become the state of Missouri, leading from the Osage hunting grounds in southwest Missouri, Arkansas and Oklahoma to the settlement in St. Louis (this would be the basic route for the St. Louis–Springfield Road, Route 66 in Missouri and modern-day Interstate 44).

The Osage profited from trade with the French and later the Spanish but were under continuing pressure to cede land, first in the mining areas around St. Genevieve and then along the Boone's Lick Trail (from St. Charles west to Franklin, Missouri, running north of the river) and along the Santa Fe Trail (from Arrow Rock and New Franklin through Independence, then southwest).

In 1803, the Louisiana Purchase added more settlement pressure. By1808, confrontations with displaced eastern tribes (the Sac and Fox, particularly) led the Osage to send one of their chiefs to Washington, D.C., to speak with Thomas Jefferson about their plight. An agreement was made in which the Osage would trade most of their land south of the Missouri River in exchange for protection and supplies. This opened up western Missouri to even more settlement. By 1825, the last remaining twenty-four-mile-wide strip of land the Osage owned in western Missouri was ceded to the U.S. government by the seventeen hundred or so remaining Osage. Quickly sold to settlers, this strip of land would include most of what would become Jackson County, Missouri, the following year.

At first, the federal government had tried to get involved in the fur trade and do business with Native Americans. The army post at Fort Osage (today the Fort Osage National Historic Site in Sibley, Missouri) was an example of the government's attempts at building a system of forts to improve relations through trade. Many Native American tribes sold goods to government-run posts, but private outfits like the American Fur Company balked at the competition. These firms eventually won the greater share of trade in Missouri. Francois Chouteau (whose uncle, Rene Auguste Chouteau, along with Pierre Laclede, founded St. Louis in 1764) represented the American Fur Company of Jacob Astor in western Missouri. In 1821, Chouteau built a home and depot on the Missouri River, where he, his wife Berenice and a few others established a small community made up mostly of French trappers and traders. Within a few years, Chouteau's landing was sending a steady stream of boats loaded with fur down the river to St. Louis. At times, there were loads as large as twenty thousand pounds being shipped in a single day.

One of the settlers in the Chouteau community was Gabriel Prudhomme. Arriving sometime in the early 1820s, Prudhomme had been a blacksmith, owned a ferry and had been granted a license to operate a tavern and grocery store. Under the Homestead Rights Act, he had claimed 257 acres that would soon be at the center of Kansas

City's development (then called the Town of Kansas). His land coincided roughly with the Missouri River as the northern border, present-day Winner Road to the south, present-day Troost Avenue on the east and present-day Broadway on the west.

In 1831, Prudhomme was killed in a bar brawl, and his land, including the natural rock ledge that would become known as Westport Landing, was eventually sold by his widow at auction (after much legal wrangling). The winning bid came from the Town of Kansas Company, consisting of many of Kansas City's and Westport's early leading citizens. The company included William Sublette, Moses G. Wilson, John C. McCoy, William Gillis, Fry P. McGee, Abraham Fonda, William M. Chick, Oliver Caldwell, George W. Tate (the auctioneer presiding over the sale), Jacob Ragan, William Collins, James Smart, Samuel C. Owens and Russell Hicks. Robert Campbell, William Evans and Henry Jobe all purchased interests in the company later, with Campbell becoming the largest landowner in the company after buying out the interests of Collins, Smart, Wilson and eventually Sublette (after his death). Many of these men were from Kentucky, though some were from Virginia and Maryland. Most of them shared a Southern cultural background. Intermarriage and business connections within this group were common too. Evans was married to the daughter of James McGee, Robert Campbell was married to Evans's daughter, McCoy married William Chick's daughter and James Smart's sister was married to Oliver Caldwell. Sublette was in the fur trade with Robert Campbell, William Chick bought his store in Westport from McCoy and Russell Hicks was Judge Samuel Owens's deputy clerk. The financial, cultural and personal ties between these founding fathers explain a good deal of their success and seeming unity of purpose in bringing trade to the frontier outpost. The bold business ethics and competiveness many of them shared may also explain why there were several lawsuits amongst them as well.

In the 1830s, Jackson County, Missouri, was only a few years old. The county seat was Independence. Established in 1827 as a trailhead town surrounded by natural springs and situated on high ground, Independence had grown quickly. There were many outfitters to help pioneers prepare for their voyages west. In 1846, *Oregon Trail* author Francis Parkman wrote of Independence:

> *The town was crowded. A multitude of shops had sprung up to furnish the emigrants and Santa Fe traders with necessaries for their journey; and there was incessant hammering and banging from a dozen blacksmiths' sheds, where the heavy wagons were being repaired and the horses and oxen shod. The streets were thronged with men, horses and mules.*

The road to Westport led through Independence. Being the county seat, Independence was bound to influence the politics and growth of their upstart, upriver rival. Independence was a slave town. The wealthy there would sometimes give slaves as wedding gifts or birthday presents. Mormon followers of Joseph Smith who came to settle in the town were driven out of Independence in part because of their antislavery views. The town's early leaders, many whose names grace the roads or schools there, were slaveholders—William Chrisman (high school), William McCoy (park) and Smallwood Noland (road), just to name a few.

In 1833, John Calvin McCoy had a two-story log structure built on land he purchased from Dr. Johnston Lykins on the north side of the wagon road that led from Independence into Indian Territory (and on to Colorado). About three miles south of the Missouri River (at the present-day northeast corner of Westport Road and Pennsylvania Avenue in Kansas City), McCoy's combination general store/tavern/home/post office became a popular stop for trappers, travelers and traders. He and his business partners, J.P. Hickman and J.H. Flournoy, had made a good choice for the business's location. In 1835, McCoy platted out a three- by four-block area around his store into lots, which he tried to sell. He ended up giving some of them away, offering lots to anyone who would start a business there.

Another tavern and hostelry owned by Daniel Yoacham was located at the northwest corner of Westport Road and Mill Street. The Yoacham family had arrived in the area from Tennessee even before the McCoys and had built a second floor on their log home so they could let out rooms to travelers on the trails.

A saddler opened a shop on one of McCoy's free lots, and other businesses soon followed, forming a loose-knit community of sparsely placed homes and businesses.

In order to keep his store supplied at first, McCoy had to have goods shipped to Independence and then brought several miles to Westport by wagon. Hoping to save the added time and expense, he convinced the captain of the riverboat *John Hancock* to come farther upriver and unload his supplies near Chouteau's community. McCoy built his own warehouse at the river and organized a group to widen and improve the road to his store and "town" (Broadway). McCoy had cleared a way to bypass the difficult crossing at the Blue River and start travel on the Santa Fe and other trails considerably west of earlier jumping-off points. Independence would eventually lose a great deal of business to Westport and Kansas City.

John C. McCoy was enterprising, locating his store one mile from the Kansas border. He was licensed to trade with Native American tribes, and many of them received annuities from the U.S. government and would spend much of this income at his store. Trappers, traders, immigrants and local gentry all found their roads led to McCoy's. Travelers would take the steamboat to Westport Landing and follow the road south through town, stopping for news, supplies and companionship, before heading into the vast prairies that lay just beyond.

In 1846, Francis Parkman spent some time in Westport waiting for a wagon train (much of it at Vogel's Tavern. near the home of Thomas Goforth, the mayor of Westport). His description of Westport contrasts with his report of Independence:

> *Westport was full of Indians, whose little shaggy ponies were tied by dozens along the houses and fences. Sac and Foxes, with shaved heads and painted faces, Shawanoes and Delawares, fluttering in calico frocks, and turbans, Wyandottes dressed like white men and a few wretched Kansas wrapped in old blankets, were strolling about the streets or lounging in and out of the shops and houses.*

Parkman simply saw Indians, whereas Westport merchants saw customers. The town grew on trade with Native Americans, Mexican traders, Mormon emigrants, French trappers and the wide variety of people who passed through on their way to and from the frontier.

Though the fur trade had been the dominant economic engine in the 1820s and was a major source of revenue in the 1830s, by the 1840s a number of other factors had come into play. Westport continued to

Westport, Missouri, circa 1859. A depiction of old Westport with a cart headed west on the Independence road. *Courtesy of the Westport Historical Society.*

see growth in trade as the Indian Removal Act was implemented, and competition heated up for contracts to distribute annuities and sell supplies to the various new arrivals. Ninety thousand Native Americans who were owed millions in annuities or payments by the government were being moved into Kansas Territory. A government contract to supply a tribe could ensure a Westport merchant's fortune.

Trade on the Santa Fe Trail and to Utah and Colorado expanded, and army posts were built to stand guard there. Some of the early forts like Fort Laramie were actually built first by traders or explorers and then used or rented by the army. In 1833, business partners William Bent and Ceran St. Verain built a fort just east of La Junta, Colorado, on the mountain branch of the Santa Fe Trail. Known as "Bent's Fort," this lonely outpost was a six-hundred-mile trek from Westport with no towns in between. Bent and St. Verain built additional forts along the United States–Mexican border; their primary trade was in buffalo robes provided by the Southern Cheyenne and Arapaho, but they also purchased furs from trappers and ponies and mules from Mexican traders. Each spring, a caravan of twenty to thirty wagons would leave the fort with goods to trade in Westport or St. Louis. Explorer John C. Fremont (son-in-law of Missouri senator and promoter of western exploration and expansion Thomas Hart Benton) used the fort as a base for some of his expeditions. Frontiersman Kit Carson was employed by Bent as a hunter and visited the fort regularly as well. During the Mexican-American War, Bent's Fort became a staging area for Colonel Stephen Watts Kearney's Army of the West.

Bent's first fort lasted until 1849. He built a second fort in 1853 and continued to anchor the far end of the trail from Westport. Even in the 1850s, the trip from Westport to Bent's Fort took over thirty days' travel time through vast stretches of wilderness. The frontier forts helped foster growth and expansion for trailhead towns like Westport, connecting markets, providing destinations or stopovers for weary travelers and making outposts along the frontier available for government use.

Contracts to supply these new posts were obtained by Westport merchants. Trappers and fur traders would lead the way into the mountains and up the rivers; forts, squatters and settlers followed behind, and Westport supplied them all. Settlement along the Platte and Missouri expanded northward. In 1837, the Platte Purchase extended the Missouri

Bent's Fort. William Bent built fortified trading posts on the Santa Fe Trail in 1833 and 1853 (pictured). *Courtesy of the Library of Congress.*

border, opening the area just across the river from Westport Landing to expansion and trade. Westport's taverns, outfitters and merchants of all types were making the most of the opportunities presented by these far-flung markets. Between 1840 and 1850, the white population in Oregon increased from 150 to 13,500. In California, the jump was from 700 to 100,000. Each spring, the trailhead towns like Independence and Westport would fill with wagons, horses and travelers preparing for the long trek west. The opening of Oregon Territory and the 1849 California gold rush closed the decade with Westport rapidly eclipsing Independence as jumping-off point for the many trails west.

Texas independence followed in 1845. Admission of Texas to the Union as a slave state led to a war with Mexico over boundaries (expansionist President Polk did little to avoid the conflict). The war with Mexico and the resulting acquisition of more lands led to another crisis and the Compromise of 1850. The Texas annexation document reserved the right to subdivide Texas into a total of five states, but the Northern states weren't about to let the status quo be upended by such a move. After a great deal of debate, California was admitted as a free state and Texas remained as one big state. New battle lines were drawn and redrawn as new territories were acquired or applied for statehood, and each new deal brought more controversy and division. Arguments concerning expansion plagued every issue. The goal of a transcontinental railroad was continually set back by sectional division over the route. Financial and political power were intertwined with the arguments concerning slavery. The war of words in the East eventually led to one of action on the frontier.

The prospects for Westport, however, had grown with a bustling economy and many families prosperous enough to build larger, more substantial homes. Some brick streets were being laid, and the permanent population included a number of successful businessmen able to invest and influence others to invest in the town's future. Churches, warehouses, saloons, hotels, breweries, blacksmith shops, grocers and trail outfitters were continually springing up throughout the booming 1840s. The rivers served to connect Kansas City and Westport with the East as the trails did with Mexico and the West.

The French community in Kansas City still maintained a small cultural influence; most notably, Berenice Chouteau (widow of Francois

Chouteau, who died in 1838 at the age of forty-one) continued to run the family business and had a fine home built on Pearl Street (near Grand and Third). Mrs. Chouteau and her family maintained a respected position in the community for several decades. She bought her son, Pierre Chouteau, a steamship, and he became known as Captain Chouteau. He served as city treasurer in Kansas City in the 1870s. Mrs. Chouteau helped raise funds to build the first Catholic church in Kansas City (St. Regis, built in 1839 at Twelfth and Broadway, where the Cathedral of the Immaculate Conception now stands). Father Bernard Donnelley oversaw the building of the church, starting a brickworks with three hundred workers he brought over from Ireland.

The social and cultural elites of Independence, Westport and Kansas City tended to know one another and had a great deal of interaction. Many had a common heritage, as most of the leaders in the 1830s and 1840s were from the South. Jackson County's elites generally lived like their Southern contemporaries, and the presence of slaves within these communities could not help but influence their political, economic and, ultimately, military destiny.

By 1850, Missouri's largest slaveholder (Jabez Smith) resided in Independence. Many of the finest homes in the town were owned by the early slaveholding families who settled and prospered there. In 1850, Hiram Young lived on Liberty Street in Independence. Young was a successful businessman who owned many slaves he had purchased on the Independence Square and put to work in his wagon shop. Many of Young's slaves learned a trade and went on to purchase their freedom, an opportunity not always offered by white slaveholders. Hiram Young was a former slave himself, who had purchased his own freedom from his master, George Young. George purchased Hiram for $800 and within a year or two allowed him to buy his freedom—for $1,500. The fact that a freed slave who helped others to gain their freedom and the largest slaveholder in the state could live within a mile of each other and both run large, successful businesses supported by slave labor is one of the strange ironies of the peculiar institution in Jackson County.

Slaveholders in the communities along the Missouri River and Boone's Lick Trail were often financially successful and influential. A look at the accounts of Jabez Smith or Hiram Young presents a picture of the interconnectedness of the finances of the entire community. Even those who didn't own slaves often borrowed money from or sold goods to those who did. In Independence, Westport and much of Jackson County, the elite owned slaves, and the rest either wanted to or felt compelled to support the leading citizens and the slave economy. (Some plantation owners hired out their slaves to work for non–slave owning farmers needing temporary help.) The complexity of relationships among slaveholding and non-slaveholding Missourians, especially in western Missouri, created a tangled web of divided loyalties that could not be sorted out throughout the Civil War and even for years afterward.

In 1850, Westport fostered numerous successful businesses and served as a base of operations for others. Wagon trains of supplies crisscrossed the West, and stagecoach service to Denver and Salt Lake City by the Westport firm of Russell, Majors and Waddell became big business. Capturing many government and private contracts, its four thousand workers, one thousand mules and forty thousand oxen kept its three thousand wagons constantly trudging back and forth along the western trails. Alexander Majors lived south of Westport, but by 1856 he had moved to State Line Road and Eighty-second Street, nearer the open prairie that could sustain the large number of horses and oxen and provide space for the wagons and people gathering for the trip west. Majors often rode at the head of wagon trains that might consist of one hundred or more wagons. Communication from the front to the rear of these trains was handled by young riders, usually teenage boys. One such rider for Majors was young Willy Cody ("Buffalo Bill" Cody, who would a few years later join the Kansas Seventh just in time to end up in the Battle of Westport). Cody became friends with another employee of Majors's firm: James Butler "Wild Bill" Hickok. (The Alexander Majors House Museum recently merged with the John Wornall House Museum to become the Wornall-Majors House Museums.)

By the late 1850s, the U.S. government was sending around $1 million a year in annuity payments to the various Native American tribes in Kansas. Over $200,000 in postal contracts came into the area as well, and the army disbursed another $2 million. It was estimated that the Santa Fe trade brought the area another $1.5 million in business. The emigrant trade added another $300,000 as well.

John B. Wornall portrait. Wornall was a successful Westport farmer and businessman. *Courtesy of the John Wornall House Museum.*

Success in Westport was not limited solely to tavern owners and western traders. In 1844, Richard Wornall bought five hundred acres south of Westport from John Calvin McCoy. He returned to Kentucky and deeded his land in Jackson County to his son, John Bristow Wornall, who lived there with his wife, Eliza, daughter of Reverend Thomas Johnson (namesake for Johnson County, Kansas, and Johnson Drive and founder of the Shawnee Indian Mission).

John B. Wornall became a successful farmer, building a large home on the land he received from his father (at present-day Sixty-first Terrace and Wornall Road). He invested his time and money in the building of the First and Second Baptist Churches in Westport. He served as president of William Jewell College and the Kansas City National Bank and as a state senator as well. His home would be used as a hospital by both sides during the Battle of Westport (it was restored by the Jackson

The Wornall Home was used as a hospital by both sides during the Battle of Westport. *Courtesy of the John Wornall House Museum.*

County Historical Society and continues to be operated as a museum, along with the Alexander Majors Home, by the J.B. Wornall House Museum Board).

Nathan Scarritt was a Methodist minister who joined Thomas Johnson at the Shawnee Indian Mission and became pastor at Westport in 1849. In 1850, he married Martha Matilda Chick (daughter of Colonel William Miles Chick) and built his home at Fortieth and Central Streets (south of Westport near Brush Creek). Scarritt's family would grow with the community, and he became involved in education (starting Westport High School), real estate and finance, as well as performing his duties as a religious leader.

John Harris came to Westport in 1831 and began buying and selling land there. He opened a store and tavern in 1846 in the log building that had originally been McCoy's store (prior to Harris, the business was owned by A.B.H. McGhee and was called the Catfish House because it served fresh catfish from the Kaw River). Later, that building burned down, and in 1852 Harris built on the same location (444 North Westport Road) a three-story brick hotel known as the Harris House Hotel. The Harris House Hotel became a celebrated stop along the trails west and a gathering place for locals as well. Harris built a home and expanded his business operations greatly with the success of his hotel. Though the hotel was torn down in 1922, John Harris's home still stands. In 1922, it was moved to its current location (4000 Baltimore Avenue) and now serves as a museum and headquarters for the Westport Historical Society. Harris also donated land for the first Baptist church in Westport at 109 Westport Road (built in 1860).

John and Henrietta Harris had several daughters, and the girls married many of the more eligible bachelors of the town. Josephine Harris married Charles E. Kearney, a successful Westport trader and Mexican-American War veteran. (They would end up living in the Harris Home later in life.) Susan Harris was married to Westport mayor and Santa Fe trader William Rodney Bernard; they lived at 3928 Pennsylvania Avenue near the home of Albert Gallatin Boone (3932 Pennsylvania), grandson of Daniel Boone. Farther down the street (4050 Pennsylvania) was the home of Thomas Goforth, first mayor of Westport and justice of the peace, and nearby was Vogel's Tavern, where Francis Parkman (author of *The Oregon Trail*) stopped while waiting for his wagon train. At 4010–12 Pennsylvania was Henry Sager's furniture shop, built in 1840. Sager made cabinets and caskets to order. At Fortieth Street and Pennsylvania Avenue, Westport's first city hall stood as early as 1860.

The Jonathan Hyatt McGhee family arrived in the Westport area in 1828, and several members became prominent citizens of the town. J.H. McGhee started a gristmill and gained a government contract to supply flour to the Indians. He added a ferry, a corn cracker and a distillery to his operations and within four years moved his family from their log home to the first brick house built in the area at Twentieth Street and Baltimore Avenue. Frye and A.B.H. McGhee would both figure in the growth of Westport and the border troubles that would signal its ultimate decline in favor of Kansas City.

William Parish built a mill at Thirty-third Street and Cleveland Avenue and later was a partner in McGhee's distillery business in the area of Roanoke. At 210 Westport Road (Westport and Central), the first brick Union Church was built on land donated in 1846 by Methodist missionary Reverend Learner Blackman Stateler. At the invitation of the Methodists, Presbyterians and Baptists also used the church until they could build their own. Across the street at 211 Westport Road was the home of Henry Clay Pate, a Westport attorney. Dr. Joel T. Morris lived at 301 Westport Road. At 312 Westport Road was the home of Duke Simpson (brother to John Harris's wife, Henrietta). Said to be one of the old town's finer homes, it fell into disrepair and was torn down in the early twentieth century. At the southeast corner of Mill Street and Westport Road was the site of Samuel C. Roby's Indian store. Next to Roby's was the shop of Phil Becker, shoemaker, and Dr. Joseph O. Boggs's Pioneer Drugstore was in the middle of the same block. James Madison Hunter came to Westport in the early 1830s and started a saddle shop on the half block between Mill Street and Pennsylvania Avenue that McCoy had given him to start a business there.

Other thriving Westport businesses included that of Albert Gallatin Boone, grandson of Daniel Boone, who bought the store at 500 Westport Road from George and William Ewing. Boone's Tavern became a popular gathering place for pro-slavery forces during the dangerous early days of Kansas settlement. Boone moved to Colorado in 1859. Cyprian Chouteau's store was next door at 501 Westport Road. A pro-Confederate newspaper called the *Border Star* was printed there until Union troops shut it down in 1861. In 1866, mountain man Jim Bridger purchased Chouteau's store. Both the Ewing-Boone and Chouteau-Bridger buildings were built within months of each other in 1850, and both remain to contest the other's status as oldest remaining commercial building in Kansas City.

Illinois senator Stephen Douglas had good intentions for the country when he offered his solution for expansion in the Kansas-Nebraska Act, though the hard consequences of his actions were to be felt for years afterward in Westport. There was strong consensus for the building of a transcontinental railroad, and many felt that a mix of private ownership and public financing would be the best way to accomplish it. The part that could not be settled was where to build it and what to do about slavery in the territories it would pass through. There were five different

Old Westport. This etching depicts the homes, businesses and people of old Westport. *Courtesy of the Westport Historical Society.*

routes proposed, each met with objections based on sectional differences. Douglas was at the center of this controversy. He hoped to gain passage of a bill that would start the rail line in Chicago, passing through Nebraska Territory. As a Northern Democrat with presidential aspirations, Douglas had to find a compromise that would be acceptable to Southern Democrats as well as Northerners. He suggested repealing the Missouri Compromise, dividing the Nebraska Territory into two territories (Kansas and Nebraska) and letting popular sovereignty determine whether the territories entered the Union as slave or free states. Douglas argued for the idea of "squatter sovereignty," basically stating that, just as the people of a state have a right to make the laws there, those living in a territory should have the right to self-determination; in particular, he promoted this right in regard to slavery. He found support from Missouri senator David Atchison, who was battling for his seat with congressman and former senator Thomas Hart Benton. Atchison favored expansion but

Stephen Douglas, the senator from Illinois whose Kansas-Nebraska Act of 1854 triggered the border war. *Courtesy of the Library of Congress.*

could not expect support from his base in western Missouri if his plans didn't extend slavery into Kansas Territory. They could only accomplish both with a change in the law.

The Kansas-Nebraska Act, rather than settling the issue, released a wave of migration and agitation into the Kansas Territory. Many in Missouri assumed that when the Kansas Territory was opened for homesteading, it would naturally follow that its near neighbors in Missouri would make up the bulk of the settlers there. All along the Missouri were comfortable communities built on an agrarian economy that used slave labor. Tobacco, hemp and other crops had succeeded cotton in importance, but much of Missouri's wealth depended on the work of those in bondage. For Missourians, the Kansas-Nebraska

Act seemed to guarantee that the state's western border would not be a magnet for runaway slaves and that succeeding generations would be able to preserve their way of life and continue its expansion into the West.

The outcome they expected was not to be. The call for settlers to establish freedom in the West rang out along the eastern seaboard. Emigrant aid societies sprang up from Boston to New Jersey. Freeing Kansas would become a cottage industry in the East and a perilous enterprise in the West. Abolitionists, as well as Free-Soilers (those who favored free-state politics for economic reasons) from the near North (Iowa, Illinois, Minnesota and Indiana) and the East, came to cast their votes for freedom.

Outraged Missourians crossed the border in force to prevent the theft of land they felt was their natural inheritance. When the 1854 Kansas-Nebraska Act was pushed through Congress, few of its proponents believed that war would be its result. As opposing forces armed themselves and faced off across the prairie, it became clear that both Kansas and Missouri would bleed. The rest of the country anxiously witnessed the struggle from afar. Jefferson's vision of a pastoral Eden peopled by gentlemen farmers was marred by the framework of slavery on which its canvas rested. Progress had been halted by the country's great conflict over direction.

At the edge of the western frontier, a mirror was held up to the nation, and the reflection drove a soul-searching people to take action to change what they saw.

As all middle ground was abandoned, the Kansas-Missouri border became a gaping wound from which blood would pour for years to come. The race to conflict seemed headlong, with little thought of the cost or who would bear it. Families on both sides of the border would be burned out or robbed, their stock stolen or killed, their fathers and sons murdered by their neighbors. Their fellow citizens, their fellow countrymen—Americans whose forefathers fought for self-determination and freedom from oppression—would fight one another over the same issues.

The Edge of the World

In 1860, Westport was the edge of the world. According to the census, Missouri had a population of nearly two million. The combined populations of the states and territories comprising Kansas, Nebraska, North and South Dakota, Oklahoma, Arizona, New Mexico, Colorado, Wyoming, Utah and Nevada numbered less than half that. A settler's journey west of town was akin to an ocean voyage or trek into a desert or jungle.

For decades after the Louisiana Purchase, the central plains had been characterized as the great American desert—a hostile and uninhabitable area. Zebulon Pike described the area as having "not a stick of timber," and geographer Edwin James, in a government survey of 1823, described the area as "almost wholly unfit for cultivation." Where the river road and eastern forests ended, settlement paused, and the new paths were blazed with an eye to the forests and rivers of the Far West, in Oregon and California.

Settlers would travel over a thousand miles through the plains and over the mountains to find "good" land out West. The cost of hauling supplies and wagons up the Missouri River by steamboat, even from St. Louis, was more than the cost of purchasing them in Independence or Westport. Thus, the little towns at the edge of the world became wealthy supplying the oxen, mules, wagons and other items necessary for the trek west.

A policy of Indian removal from their eastern homelands to the "desert lands" of the West led to a string of forts springing up along the western frontier to deal with the conflicts between settlers and the tribes being moved in, as well as established tribes who already lived in these areas. Forts Leavenworth and Scott (Kansas), Fort Gibson (Oklahoma), old Fort Kearney (Nebraska), Fort Smith (Arkansas), Forts Croghan (Council Bluffs) and Des Moines (Iowa), Fort Abercrombie (North Dakota), Fort Ripley (Minnesota) and dozens of others formed a line separating the settled areas from native lands and served to police the various populations beyond the edges of settlement.

By the 1850s, the line was wavering. Settlers pressed ever westward—for gold in California, for gold in Colorado, for land anywhere it could be had. Proponents of Manifest Destiny, like Jackson County's William Gilpin (later the governor of Colorado), argued vehemently against earlier writers' mischaracterizations of the central plains. He claimed these lands were a virtual paradise. There was sufficient water to grow a sea of grass and feed millions of buffalo; surely it could sustain enlightened farmers raising grain and cattle. A vision grew of the eastern states connecting with the new territories in the Far West by telegraph wire and rail, while free settlers filled the heartland.

There were fortunes to be made in these territories, and Westport traders vied to get their share, especially in Kansas. Indian lands that treaties said would be theirs as long as rivers flowed and grass grew were facing a man-made drought. Squatters' camps sprung up on more and more of the lands reserved for Native Americans. The slightest rumor that a tribe would be selling its land (willingly or not) brought speculators of every stripe, from pioneers just looking for a place to put down roots to developers sent from eastern states to snatch up any parcel they could get their hands on. The race to build new towns, states and economic empires was in high gear.

Expansion of slavery and Indian policy were core conflicts in the 1850s, but a third issue ranked equally in the amount of attention it received from the town fathers of Kansas and Westport: railroads. A town on a major line had a connection to the world, a way to market its products and purchase manufactured goods. The ease of access the railroad could bring often meant investment, a larger population and an increase in land values. In the 1850s, there was a great political and economic battle being fought to build a transcontinental railroad. Frontier towns like St. Joseph and Westport competed to gain rail service but often lacked the political influence to effect the direction of progress. Larger cities like Chicago and St. Louis would become railroad hubs and would drive debate in their state legislatures on which routes to consider. State senators and representatives in Washington would use their political capital to influence the railroads or influence their fellows in favor of one plan or another. The whole process was beyond the control of any one person, so alliances, tradeoffs and schemes held hostage the future of all.

In 1856, the Kansas Town Company bought a printing press in St. Louis and started a newspaper called the *Enterprise* (an organ meant mostly to promote the town to the railroads and vice versa). Within a year, they sold the paper to Robert Thompson Van Horn. As editor, Van Horn was a tireless champion of the town. A chamber of commerce was formed the same year, prompting a similar agenda to that of the newspaper. The Town of Kansas passed a bond issue to sell bonds that would be traded for stock shares in a rail line, any rail line that would further connect the city with the East. A second bond issue came before

The Far West. Shooting buffalo on the line of the Kansas Pacific Railroad. *Courtesy of the Library of Congress.*

the county, and many more votes were cast in favor of the levy than the town had in eligible voters. The proponents of rail would get the vote they wanted—one way or another.

There was a steady focus on the goal of bringing rail service to Kansas City. The city fathers had a clear vision of the economic benefit and loss at stake. The competition to be on the proposed transcontinental railroad was fierce and became closely tied to sectional disputes over the expansion of slavery. Influence in Washington was sought and deals struck by one community after another as speculators tried to induce or cajole their representatives into bringing home the prize. State politics would also influence where funding for projects would go, just as competition between St. Louis and Kansas City interests continue to affect Missouri growth and direction. By 1860, Missouri would have over eight hundred miles of rail line, and by 1870 that number would more than double. But in the 1850s, the fear of being left behind by these engines of change was palpable, and Westport and the Town of Kansas (later renamed Kansas City) made concerted efforts to get on board.

The Kansas-Nebraska Act of 1854 has been credited by many historians as being the pivotal event that set the Civil War in motion. The three great issues of expansion of slavery, the "Indian question" and the great political/economic rivalry between North and South all came together in the Kansas-Nebraska Act. Each issue seemed tied to progress for the country, and the act seemed to challenge everyone involved to take action in order to protect his or her own interests. By turning over the question of slavery in the territories to popular sovereignty, Congress set a proxy war in motion. Pro-slavery Missourians saw group after group of antislavery or abolitionist settlers come in through Westport. In Kansas, settlers from Missouri had staked out land and were moving slowly in, but waves of settlers from points farther east began crashing on the plains. Emigrant aid societies were formed in Connecticut, Massachusetts, Pennsylvania, New York and New Jersey, providing financial backing for settlers who would vote to make Kansas a free state. A hotel (Gillis House Hotel) was purchased by the emigrant aid society, and passages to the west, as well as supplies for settlement, were also provided for the emigrants. These groups didn't always get the friendliest welcome from the pro-slavery majority in Westport or Kansas City as they stepped off the steamboats at Westport Landing. But there was a great deal of support for their work from the eastern aid societies as financial support flowed east to west to the settlers in Kansas Territory.

The pressure of the swelling white population also was felt by the Native American tribes as schemes to part them from their land were perpetrated. Many tribes were bought out or pushed out, sent to Oklahoma or farther west. Missourians, who had transplanted to Kansas with their slaves, were under enormous pressure to either free them or leave the territory. The battle for control of Kansas Territory was between North and South, East and West, Native Americans and whites, all trying to gain control of the future and bend it to their will.

In 1860, Westport had a population of around 1,800, of which 85 families owned some 420 slaves. Around half of the slave-owning families lived on farms, while the other half lived in town. Wealth alone didn't define slaveholders; one of the wealthiest men in Westport at that time was Charles E. Kearney, owner of 1 slave. Thomas Polk, who also lived in town but was not nearly as well off as Kearney, owned 42 slaves. Farmer Jesse Porter had 20 slaves, while John Harris, owner of the Harris House Hotel, had 16 and Peter H. Smith, owner of the Smith Hotel (similar in size to the Harris House), owned only 2 slaves.

Slavery in Missouri had survived despite the difference in climate and growing conditions. Large-scale plantations and cotton production had not followed the slave culture into Missouri. The adapted version was perhaps worse in that no perceived economic necessity like that in the South had driven the expansion. The hope that slavery would fail on its own had lost momentum with the widespread use of the cotton gin ("gin" was short for engine), which made large-scale production of short-staple cotton practical. As a result, the number of slaves had more than tripled in the first half of the nineteenth century, and the South was producing two-thirds of the world's cotton by 1860.

Pro-slavery towns like Leavenworth, Atchison and Kickapoo were platted just as antislavery towns like Topeka, Lawrence and Emporia were built to counter them. Speculators bought land, platted towns and sold lots to investors in the East, appealing to their avarice as well as their political sympathies. Indian lands were purchased, often by pitting factions within a tribe against one another through bribes or false promises. Many of these "deals" were sanctioned by Federal authority, so new lands continued to become available for private use. Many of the new Kansas towns produced their own newspapers, promoting the political and economic aspirations of the towns' leading citizens. Subscriptions to some of these papers outnumbered the population of the towns, as many were held by supporters in the East. There were twenty-seven newspapers in Kansas in 1861 but only ten towns with populations in excess of five hundred.

Daniel Read Anthony (the brother of civil rights leader Susan B. Anthony) was editor of the popular *Leavenworth Conservative*, and his fiery rhetoric helped sow division both in the territory and back East. Although divisions over slavery existed from the country's inception, Kansas presented a perfect setting for those with radical feelings on either side of the issue to act on. Arguments in the popular press over events in Kansas did little to soften the tenor of the warring factions. Like moths to the flame, men like James Lane, William Quantrill and James Montgomery came to Kansas to join the fray. There were Free-Soilers, squatter sovereigns, Blue Lodgers and every stripe of radical idealist mixed in with speculators, con artists and salt-of-the-earth pioneers—all in a territory that would be harmed greatly by a lack of money with the Panic of 1857, the drought of 1860 and collapse of the land speculation market that followed.

A territory that had few slaves and was ill suited agriculturally for a slave economy strangely ended up becoming the focal point for the opposing forces competing over the expansion of slavery and the future of the nation.

The town of Lawrence, Kansas (thirty miles west of Westport), was named after Amos Adams Lawrence, a prominent Massachusetts abolitionist. Like many early towns in eastern Kansas, Lawrence was established by settlers who opposed the spread of slavery in the territory. Many of the residents' views went well beyond partisan politics. The abolitionist movement was a great moral cause, and with it came men who used the great moral rationalization of the end justifies the means. Lawrence was headquarters, at one time or another, to John Brown, Jim Lane, James Montgomery, Charles Jennison and William Quantrill. Turncoats, opportunists and zealots looking for followers, these men's intolerance and venality colored the conversation and drowned out civil discourse between the opposing sides.

Missourians, at the behest of Senator Atchison and pro-slavery leader Benjamin Franklin Stringfellow, had flocked across the border and voted for pro-slavery candidates to the territorial legislature. Many used violence and intimidation to prevent free-staters from succeeding. Governor Reeder nullified the first vote of March 30, 1855, as the number of ballots cast far outnumbered the number of eligible voters. The May 22, 1855 election was also skewed by Missourians, organized by Atchison and Stringfellow, who had offered a free ferry ride, a dollar per day and plenty of liquor to those who would cross the border and vote. Stringfellow was a lawyer and had served in the Missouri House of Representatives. He served as Missouri's attorney general from 1845 to 1849. After moving to Weston, Missouri (across the border from Leavenworth, Kansas), in 1853, he started a newspaper called the *Squatter Sovereign* and promoted the establishment of "Blue Lodges" to raise money and encourage supporters of slavery to settle in Kansas and counter the free-state movement. Stringfellow advocated violence against the abolitionists in Kansas. Governor Anthony Reeder (first governor of Kansas Territory) went to Washington to try to convince President Franklin Pierce not to accept the results of the second election. While there, he gave a speech decrying Stringfellow and his fellow "border ruffians," coining the term that was to be used so freely to describe Missourians. On July 2, 1855, Stringfellow confronted Reeder over his comments and struck him, knocking him to the ground. Reeder was fired by President Pierce in August 1855.

Abolitionists in Kansas were outraged by the results of the election. The border ruffians from Missouri argued that they had more right to vote on the future of Kansas than a bunch of hirelings from Boston who had just stepped off the boat in Kansas City. Men like John Brown and his sons were drawn to this conflict. Lawrence seethed over the fraud perpetrated by the Missourians during the election. The pro-slavery faction moved quickly to consolidate a hold on the state and end the debate. Laws were passed to prevent even speaking for abolition. Helping a runaway slave was punishable by death, and the governor was explicitly denied the right of pardon in such cases. The "bogus legislature" forced the hand of the abolitionists in Kansas. If they weren't willing to fight for their beliefs, this legislature would not allow them to speak or live according to them.

On May 21, 1856, a group of over eight hundred border ruffians came to Lawrence to "assist" Deputy U.S. Marshal Fain and County Sheriff Jones in enforcing Kansas law there. The group's plan seemed to have been to try to force Lawrence residents into a fight by arresting several citizens, disarming the town and destroying the newspaper offices and hotel. The town stoically stood by while the posse sacked homes, burned businesses and tossed printing presses and books into the Kaw River.

On May 19 and 20 in Washington, D.C., Senator Charles Sumner gave a speech known as the "Crime against Kansas" speech, in which he ridiculed fellow senator Andrew Butler of South Carolina and his support of slavery. Sumner mimicked Butler's speech and mannerisms (which were due in part to a stroke Butler had suffered). Butler's nephew, Preston Brooks, was incensed by the speech and felt that Sumner's insult had to be answered. He consulted South Carolina representative Laurence M. Keitt, intending to challenge Sumner to a duel, but Keitt convinced him that Sumner wasn't worthy of such a challenge, which was reserved for social equals. On May 22, Brooks attacked Sumner in the Senate chamber, beating him so severely with his cane that it broke. Sumner didn't return to his duties as senator for another three years. The Northern press castigated Brooks, while the Southern press upheld him as the honorable defender of a kinsman who could scarce defend himself. The beating of Sumner and the events in Kansas were linked in the popular press by the editor of the *New York Tribune*, Horace Greeley, who wrote of bleeding Sumner and bleeding Kansas.

In response to the attack on Lawrence, John Brown and his sons captured a group of seven suspected pro-slavery men in Osawatomie and hacked five of them to death with a broadsword. He and his sons lived in Lawrence and took part in much of the fighting in the early days of the conflict, which included attacks and reprisals all along the border. From 1854 through 1858, the political and military battles that occurred in Kansas became the food for the popular press. No single issue of the times drew so much printer's ink. Four separate constitutions were placed before the people of Kansas; two (1855 Topeka, 1857 Lecompton) were

John Brown, who led violent attacks on slavery supporters in Kansas, was hanged in 1859. *Courtesy of the Library of Congress.*

sent to Congress to be approved. The Lecompton Constitution was endorsed by President James Buchanan but opposed by Republicans and Northern Democrats, including Stephen Douglas. This Democratic split set the stage for the 1860 Republican victory. In Wyandotte, Kansas, a free-state constitution was approved and sent to Washington on October 4, 1859. Kansas was finally admitted as a free state on January 29, 1861. At long last, Missouri had lost control of its neighbor's, and to some degree its own, destiny.

As the political struggle tilted in favor of Kansas and the abolitionists, jayhawking expeditions across the border to free slaves and confiscate

Senator James Lane led forces that burned and looted much of western Missouri. *Courtesy of the Library of Congress.*

property of slave owners became more and more common. Now groups of men on both sides of the border attacked and burned farms, homes and towns in a terrible cycle of violence. A steady stream of wagons headed past Westport again, this time carrying loot from Missouri homes. After the 1860 elections and violent spring that followed, Senator Jim Lane and Colonel Charles Jennison raided towns up and down the Missouri border. Following Lane's infamous attack on Osceola, Missouri, in September 1861 (Lane executed nine private citizens after a drumhead court and then burned all but three homes in the town of several thousand), Lane was credited with ordering his men to "root out anything disloyal, from a

Jennison's Jayhawkers were as notorious for pillage and murder in Missouri as Quantrill was in Kansas. *Courtesy of the Library of Congress.*

Shanghai rooster to a Durham cow" as they loaded nearly every wagon in town with loot to send across the border. The transition to war along the border was practically seamless, as both sides had been in armed conflict for nearly six years.

The town of Westport's attempts to stay neutral, much like those of the state of Missouri, were doomed to failure. There was too much at stake, and passions ran too strong. The combination of political expediency and economic pragmatism (the abolitionists had lots of money to spend and political backing in Washington) led many businessmen in Westport (at least tacitly) to support the Federal authority.

Most of the early leaders had Southern backgrounds and allegiances, but government contracts, licenses to trade with the Indian tribes and even transporting the mail was a political game, and Westport's businessmen had to play to it to survive. As the troubles in Kansas grew, so did the population of free-state supporters and businessmen. Some, like Kersey Coates, had come as representatives of emigrant aid societies, while others had simply come to take advantage of the financial opportunities the growing population across the border provided. Though the majority of citizens still had sympathetic ties with the South, there was little hope of turning the tide of change against the free-state movement. The financial and political power in the East was becoming more and more vested in control of the West and of the political situation there.

Another factor, beyond economics and geographic ties, in the town of Westport was the great moral arguments being made by the newcomers. The abolitionist movement was growing in influence both locally and nationally. Leaders of the movement like William Lloyd Garrison and Frederick Douglass, through their speeches and writings, placed the debate before the public. The dispute over slavery in Kansas framed the issue clearly, as the nation witnessed the lengths to which both sides were willing to go to advance their visions of the future. The national debate had seen a series of shocks throughout the 1850s: The Fugitive Slave Act as part of the Compromise of 1850 allowed pursuit and capture of escaped slaves in free states. Publication of *Uncle Tom's Cabin* in 1852 drew a great sympathetic response as Harriet Beecher Stowe painted a picture of the corrupting nature of human bondage on those who participated in it. The Kansas-Nebraska Act in 1854 created the stage for the years of bloodshed along the Kansas-Missouri border. In 1857, the Dred Scott case was finally decided, denying the most basic civil rights to Negro slaves. In 1859, John Brown made his infamous raid on Harpers Ferry, Virginia, attempting to start a slave rebellion. Southerners recoiled at the thought of losing the engine of their economy (slave property that had increased continually in value) and of a large population of freed slaves that might seek revenge for the life they'd endured under slavery.

In 1860, Missouri had 114,000 slaves (according to the state census), whom the state auditor had valued in excess of $44 million. Debts were secured, income was produced, status was maintained and fortunes depended on this "property." Whether to free the slaves should have been a simple moral issue in a country dedicated to individual rights and freedoms. But how to free them was a terribly complex political and economic problem. The challenge in Missouri came in trying to convince a group of people, including many wealthy and influential citizens of the state, to *give* away $44 million in "property" without offering any financial compensation or a comparable labor force that could replace the freed slaves. Men like Henry Washington Younger (former state senator and father to Cole, Bob and Jim Younger of the James-Younger Gang) and Solomon Young (grandfather to Harry Truman) had built large and successful farms and businesses using slave labor. Their past and future success, and that of their children, depended on slave labor. Even those who only owned a few slaves, like Preacher Robert James (father of Frank and Jesse James) or Reverend Thomas Johnson (Methodist minister who ran the Shawnee Indian Mission), were bound by and to the institution. These men faced financial ruin, cultural upheaval and violent overthrow of their way of life. It is not surprising that many fought to keep their power and position with the ballot and that some would fight to keep it with the bullet. The stakes were high, and in Kansas the game was ending. Free-state men finally outnumbered the pro-slavery faction in sufficient numbers to ensure the elections. Kansas would enter the Union with $100,000 in debt, stricken by a two-year drought and in a state of undeclared war with its neighbor—but as a free state. Kansans would receive over $1 million in assistance from aid societies in the East in order to make it through the winter of 1860–61. There would never be another slave state admitted to the Union, and with the fight over Kansas ended, a new, more ominous, fight was about to begin.

A Family Fight

There is no winning in a war amongst brothers, a war within family. In Westport and Kansas City, the 1860 elections marshaled in a new era of division that would test the bonds of the towns' leading families. Westport and Kansas City had survived the previous decade's violence and even prospered to some degree from the trade that resulted from it.

But now, the balancing act that the leading men there had performed so adeptly was no longer possible. Dr. Lykins had written an editorial in Van Horn's *Journal of Commerce* warning of the dire consequences of secession. Lykins's wife was a Southerner and was very outspoken in her views, a trait that would eventually lead to her expulsion from the state. The political agitation that preceded the election was heightened within the community as the old arguments kept being dredged up. The October 1859 raid by John Brown on Harpers Ferry, his hanging in December and the subsequent highly charged political campaign of 1860 all added volume to the discourse. Through many difficult years, pro-slavery leaders like John Calvin McCoy, J.H. McGhee and Albert Gallatin Boone had been able to work in concert with new men like Kersey Coates and Robert Thompson Van Horn to advance the interests of the community. Perhaps seeing the writing on the wall, Boone sold his store in 1859 and moved to Colorado. Those with pro-slavery views who chose to remain witnessed terrific changes in the commercial and political order of the town. Men like E.M. McGee and John Calvin

President Abraham Lincoln received only 10 percent of the vote in Missouri in 1860. *Courtesy of the Library of Congress.*

McCoy would find their positions in society reduced from one of trust to one of suspicion or assumed guilt.

Kansas City (also known as the Town of Kansas) had been rapidly growing up to rival Westport, but many of the leading citizens had financial concerns in both. The rivalry was mostly friendly, and often the two communities acted in concert. Many Westport merchants had property in both towns, with warehouses where they shipped or received goods along the banks of the Missouri River.

The first signs of real change came with the fall elections in 1860. Abraham Lincoln would only garner 10 percent of the vote in the state of Missouri and even less in Westport. In Kansas City, there might have been no votes for the winning candidate had not Colonel Coates armed an escort for Lincoln supporters and led them to the polls.

The pro-slavery majority in these towns was simply out of step with the sources of prosperity that had helped build them. Most of the new settlers heading into Kansas Territory were no longer sympathetic to the South. The new element in Kansas City was aligned with the business interests that controlled the railroads, was financing much of Kansas settlement and supported the Union.

It was the old guard of Westport that would see its world turned upside down, as men of influence and power faced loss of position as the Federal authority and its representatives realigned with the new political order under the Republican Party.

Missouri was divided sharply over the issue of slavery, but a majority still opposed secession. When other Southern states seceded, there were still many in Missouri who hoped to carry on a policy of neutrality.

After President Abraham Lincoln's election, states began to secede. Seven states had seceded before Lincoln took office. Lincoln luckily avoided an assassination plot on his way to Washington and was sworn in on March 4, 1861. In March 1861, newly elected Missouri governor Claiborne Jackson asked the legislature to order a convention to consider Missouri's relationship with the Federal government. Though Jackson had run as a "Douglas" Democrat and supporter of popular sovereignty, he was clearly pro-slavery, and it is likely he hoped the convention would deliver a vote for secession. Former Missouri governor Sterling Price was elected presiding officer of the Missouri State Convention on February 28, 1861. The representatives chosen for the convention were mostly Constitutional Unionists and Douglas Democrats who supported the Union, with slavery and expansion a matter to be decided by popular sovereignty, despite the problems in Kansas. The vote went ninety-eight to one against secession.

The convention also declared that Missouri should not provide arms or men to either side in the conflict. On April 12, 1861, the war began in earnest with the attack on Fort Sumter. A few days later, on April 20, 1861, a mob of pro-Confederate men took over the Federal arsenal in Liberty, Missouri.

On the other side of the state, Francis Preston "Frank" Blair, a prominent St. Louis politician with close ties to the Lincoln administration (his brother Montgomery Blair was Lincoln's postmaster general), was working hard to keep Missouri in the Union. Secessionists were on the move and were spread throughout the state, not just in the west. St. Louis

Major General Sterling Price led the 1864 Confederate raid of Missouri and Kansas. *Courtesy of the Library of Congress.*

Francis Blair of St. Louis was a key player in the 1861 secession crisis in Missouri. *Courtesy of the Library of Congress.*

and Pike Counties on the eastern border held over eight thousand slaves between them, and many people there supported secession. Captain Nathaniel Lyon, a staunch abolitionist from Connecticut, had been transferred to St. Louis and, with Blair's support, would soon be a key figure in Missouri's future. Governor Jackson had sent the Missouri Home Guard militia to the outskirts of St. Louis, ostensibly to drill and prepare to defend the state against invasion. On April 24, 1861, Captain Lyon entered the home guard camp in disguise and obtained firsthand knowledge of a plan to attack the arsenal at St. Louis. Upon his return, Lyon secured the arsenal and shipped arms and ammunition across the Mississippi to safer ground in Illinois. Captain Lyon had discovered that siege cannons (as requested from Confederate president Jefferson Davis by Governor Jackson) had been sent to the camp by the Confederacy to help take the arsenal.

With a militia made up mostly of six thousand new German-American recruits, Lyon surrounded and disarmed the camp of some six hundred men and then paraded them through the streets of St. Louis. A pro-Southern (and anti-German) crowd gathered in the streets; someone fired a gun and a riot ensued. Seventy-five people in the crowd (including women and children) were wounded and twenty-eight were killed. (Three militia and two Federal troops were also killed.) This event, known as the Camp Jackson Affair, served to polarize Missourians further and to spur recruiting and organization efforts on both sides. General William S. Harney (commander of the Department of the West) tried to secure a truce. The Price Harney Agreement would keep Missouri neutral as long as it didn't provide arms or men to either side in the conflict. Neither the agreement nor Harney's position as commander would last. The radical Republicans were on the ascent. General Harney was called to Washington. On the way, Harney was taken prisoner by Confederate soldiers at Harpers Ferry, Virginia, where General Robert E. Lee offered him a post in the Confederate army. Harney refused and was allowed to continue his trip to Washington, only to be relieved of his position upon arrival there (an action precipitated by the Blair faction that Lincoln later described as one of the greatest mistakes of his administration).

Frank Blair had used his connections to gain access to Lincoln and convinced him to appoint John C. Fremont as department commander

General William S. Harney was commander of the Department of the West in 1861. *Courtesy of the Library of Congress.*

in Missouri. Fremont had been the Republican Party's first candidate for president and was a solid abolitionist and unionist. General Lyon had been appointed temporary commander of the Department of the West until Fremont could take his place. With General Harney forced out by Blair, Jackson and Price attempted once again to negotiate a truce with the new Federal authority. They arranged to meet with General Lyon and Francis Blair on June 11, 1861, at the Planter's House Hotel in St. Louis. Price and Jackson hoped to reach a truce while retaining control of the state militia to counter Lyon's forces. Exasperated with the proceedings, and with the very idea that a governor would try to dictate terms to the Federal government, Lyon ended the meeting abruptly, tersely saying, "This means war." Price and Jackson fled, commandeering a locomotive.

They burned bridges behind them, and at one point Price personally tore down telegraph wires, fearing Lyon would pursue them or wire ahead for forces to arrest them. The legislature fled before Union forces to Boonville and then to southwest Missouri. At Neosho, a vote for secession was made by the legislators who had made it that far on October 30. It was signed by Governor Jackson on October 31, but it has since been argued that there were insufficient numbers there to make a quorum, meaning the secession was not legal. The Confederate States of America did accept the action in Neosho, though, and Missouri became a Confederate state on November 28, 1861.

Robert Van Horn had been elected mayor of Kansas City in April 1861, but the state legislature had quickly divested the mayor and city council of police powers. Secretly traveling to St. Louis, Van Horn sought help from Blair and Lyon. He received a major's commission in the Enlisted Missouri Militia and was introduced to Captain W.E. Prince of the regular army, who was stationed at Fort Leavenworth. When Major Van Horn returned in May, he found the situation in town so volatile that he felt compelled to request that a detachment from Fort Leavenworth be sent to keep order until he could enroll a Union battalion from the townsmen. Men and guns were loaded on a steamboat at Fort Leavenworth on June 9, 1861. A pro-Confederate mob met the troops at the levee, but Captain Prince ordered his men to fix bayonets and disembark. The crowd dispersed as the force (complete with horse-drawn cannons) worked its way up Main Street. Secessionist forces moved to Westport and Independence, where the first action took place at Rock Creek between Captain Prince's forces and a group of secessionists, ending in three dead and two wounded.

Van Horn's battalion of United States Volunteer Reserve Corps took over duty from the regular troops on June 24, 1861. Organized into German, Irish and American companies under Major R.T. Van Horn, with surgeon Joshua Thorne in charge of the hospital, the force's first headquarters were on Walnut Street between Eleventh and Twelfth Streets; they moved shortly thereafter to the southwest corner of Tenth and Central Streets. The foundation of the Coates House Hotel immediately to the east was boarded over to serve as a cavalry stable. The headquarters was fortified with breastworks (chest-level defenses), and a large iron cannon and two smaller howitzers were placed there. The men drilled on Broadway between Tenth and Twelfth Streets and practiced maneuvers on the hills on either side of Broadway south of Twelfth Street. The quartermaster's stables were across the road from the fort on Tenth Street, and the commissary warehouse was on the riverbank west of Broadway. The hospital was established under Dr. Thorne at the Farmer's Hotel on Grand Avenue near Sixteenth Street (where it remained throughout the war).

Missouri's secession was eventually recognized by the Confederacy but not by the U.S. government. Militias, Federal troops, gangs of armed men and bands of robbers threatened much of the state as the elected legislature had abandoned Jefferson City and left the people to their own devices.

In the absence of governor and legislature, a new state government was appointed by the delegates to the earlier convention, with Judge Hamilton Gamble at its head. Missouri now had two governments of questionable legitimacy, neither of which controlled the entire state, and each was recognized by one national government and denied by the other. Price and Jackson had retreated to the southwest corner of the state and made an uneasy alliance with General Benjamin McCulloch's Confederate Arkansas forces. Extending his pursuit far from his supply base, and attacking Price with insufficient numbers, General Lyon was killed at the Battle of Wilson's Creek near Springfield on August 3, 1861. Confederate victories in southwest Missouri at Carthage, Wilson's Creek and Dry Wood Creek forced Federal troops north to focus on holding the Missouri Valley. Price's victory at Lexington (September 13–20, 1861) rallied pro-slavery Missourians to support the cause and dampened enthusiasm among Union supporters in the western half of the state. Along the Missouri-Kansas border, Senator Jim Lane followed Price's march north from a distance, burning and looting his way up the border. By the time Major Van Horn could link up with the Kansans in Harrisonville, most of the town's businesses had been looted by Lane's troops. Van Horn was ordered to Lexington; he was captured there and then released in a prisoner exchange. Having sworn not to take up arms against the Confederacy in order to obtain his release, Van Horn left military service and returned to being an advocate for Kansas City and its future growth. John Calvin McCoy's son, Spencer McCoy, would die

General John C. Fremont was fired by Lincoln for his heavy-handed policies in Missouri. *Courtesy of the Library of Congress.*

at the Battle of Springfield. Archibald Yoacham (son of Daniel) would die at the Battle of Wilson's Creek (Archibald Street in Westport was named in memoriam). The early years of the war would be hard on many of the old guard, as they would lose family and positions as the war ground on.

Commissioned as a major general, John C. Fremont intended to make the secessionists in Missouri pay dearly for their opposition. After Lyon's death at Wilson's Creek, Fremont declared martial law and began emancipating slaves and confiscating other private property of Missourians who supported secession. Fremont failed to control his generals, who in turn failed to control the severity of the actions of their men. General John Pope in northeast Missouri probably created more

General John Pope's Draconian policies fueled rebellion in Missouri. *Courtesy of the Library of Congress.*

secessionists than he defeated, feeding and housing his army at the public's expense, punishing the civilian population (regardless of whether they were pro-Union or Confederate) for guerrillas' actions. Under Fremont, a state that had supported the Union in spite of its Southern connections and slave economy was being pushed toward rebellion. President Lincoln asked Fremont to revise his orders, but Fremont refused, sending his wife to Washington to try to plead his case to Lincoln. On November 2, 1861, Lincoln relieved Fremont of command and revoked Fremont's proclamation of martial law.

Fremont was replaced in Missouri by General David Hunter, who was promptly moved west and replaced by General Henry Halleck, followed by General Samuel R. Curtis, General John M. Schofield and finally General William S. Rosecrans, as various command arrangements for the trans-Mississippi and western theater were tried. Fremont had failed to contain Price and had lost the initiative with the loss of Lyon. However, this state of affairs didn't last. Price lacked the arms and supplies to maintain his force in central Missouri through the winter of 1861–62. Many potential recruits had to be turned away after Lexington for lack of materials to sustain them. Price turned south, but Fremont's army stayed near Rolla, gathering in strength. Citizens of Westport and Kansas City had to endure rumors and reports that gave no true indication of their future. Dueling militias, dueling armies and dueling governments left the towns on edge.

Guerrilla groups like that of William Clarke Quantrill had already formed during the border wars, crossing over for reprisals or after loot. The war gave these groups an air of legitimacy as they resisted the occupation of Missouri by Federal troops put in place by the elected legislature. Because of the peculiar circumstances of Missouri's dueling governments, the guerrillas were looked upon alternately as commissioned troops of the Confederacy and defenders of the state from a foreign invader or as common criminals guilty of treason and subject to execution on sight. Between March 6 and 8, 1862, the Confederate defeat at the Battle of Pea Ridge, in Arkansas, solidified Union control of Missouri, and the formal Confederate army was driven from Missouri. However, in 1862 and 1863, guerrilla groups, numbering a few hundred young men, continued to keep thousands of Federal troops occupied, futilely trying to defend targets and to find guerrillas in the thick underbrush and close-knit communities of the river counties. The unsettled state of affairs in Missouri was to continue throughout the war and for years afterward. St. Louis, and to some degree traffic along the Mississippi, was secured, but guerrilla activity would continuously threaten communications and commerce across the state.

Separating the Rebels from the civilian population in parts of the state was like separating sugar from salt. Union commanders charged with keeping the lines of communication open and protecting commerce were under increasing pressure to take action against the guerrillas. By 1863, a number of steps had been taken to limit the ability of the guerrillas to obtain support from the civilian populace. Neighbors were coerced by Federal troops to inform on families and friends of the guerrillas. Militia from Kansas, led by Jim Lane and Colonel Charles Jennison, went from farm to farm and town to town on both sides of the border, seeking Rebels or their sympathizers. Those who had so much as spoken in favor of the South or against the occupying forces were liable to imprisonment, exile or worse. Southerners and slave owners in the river communities were forced to put up large bonds to remain and do business. Many would lose their homes and businesses, in spite of every effort to comply, as frustration with the guerrillas' success mounted.

Kansas City was occupied territory, with Camp Union and the many troops, both Federal and state, that were there. The citizens of Westport who owned slaves or were in any way thought to be connected to the secessionist Rebels were under constant threat of arrest. Pro-Union citizens were in little better position, as out-of-state troops distrusted them, and many of their neighbors were still sympathetic to the guerrillas who threatened the roads and farms surrounding town. Suspicion and dissent within the community strained relations, despite the familiar bonds that had kept it together through the 1850s.

Of the surviving founders of Kansas City, several were touched directly by the war. William Gillis had a large home and farm, both built and run by slave labor, at Twenty-seventh and Holly Streets. During the war, the property was looted by Kansas border ruffians, and Gillis was forced to move farther into town (Fourth and Locust) just as Nathan Scarritt had left Westport for Kansas City out of fear of attack by Missouri guerrillas.

A witch-hunt mentality had set in concerning the guerrillas, and it would only get worse. Under General Order Number 10, family members or friends believed to have aided the guerrillas were rounded up and jailed, pending exile from their homes. In June 1863, a raid on the outskirts of Westport in which a guerrilla group led by Lieutenant George Todd attacked a 150-man detachment of the Ninth Kansas Cavalry, killing twenty and wounding several more, set a series of actions in motion that would lead from one tragedy to another. General Thomas Ewing had already been arresting female relatives of the guerrillas under the pretext that they were spying for the groups. A group of young women who were relatives of the guerrillas were rounded up and held on the second floor of an unsteady building near Fourteenth Street and Grand Avenue in downtown Kansas City (approximately where the Sprint Center is located today). The third floor of the building was George Caleb Bingham's art studio, and the first floor was being used by a local merchant for storage. A group of women of easy virtue had been living in the basement of the building, and soldiers from a guard post next door had broken down one of the walls to gain easy access to the basement. The loss of support caused the upper floor to sag, and General Ewing was notified on the morning of August 13, 1863, that the building had become unstable. (The women had complained of the building swaying in the wind for some time before the foundation had been weakened.) The merchant on the first floor removed his stock into the street for fear of collapse, but the prisoners were left in the building. The building collapsed that afternoon, killing four of the girls (most of the prisoners were teenagers) and severely injuring the rest. Among those killed were a sister of William "Bloody Bill" Anderson and a sister and cousin of Cole Younger. Anderson had three sisters in the building collapse. The youngest, ten-year-old Mary Anderson, tried to jump out a window of the building, but the iron ball and chain attached to her ankle prevented her escape, breaking both her legs and leaving her a cripple for the rest of her life. Her story, like those of many of the people who suffered on both sides of the border, has been largely untold or under told, as many narratives tend to bolster the innocence of one side or another (though evidence clearly points to brutal excesses being sanctioned by leadership on both sides of the conflict).

Though the guerrillas had been planning an attack on Lawrence before this event, it is a reasonable assumption that the news of this loss, received as they were gathered to plot their next move, gave added impetus to the plan. Over 300 guerrillas attacked Lawrence (thirty miles west of Westport) on August 21, 1863. They crossed the border in the open, unchallenged by Federal troops, at Aubrey, Kansas, and proceeded some forty miles beyond and behind the Federal line of defense placed there. They looted, burned homes and buildings and killed over 150 men and boys. There is little doubt that the loot to be had in Lawrence was a motivation for many of Quantrill's men, and for Quantrill himself, but they also came with a list of homes and men they wished to wreak particular vengeance on for purported crimes committed against Missouri. Quantrill's men were under orders not to attack women, Negroes or children, but they did not exempt old men or adolescent boys. Quantrill's men, after all, were largely teenagers and twenty-somethings themselves. Quantrill was twenty-three at the start of the war; Bloody Bill was twenty-two, Frank James was seventeen and Frank's younger brother, Jesse, was fourteen. The "troops" that headed into Kansas included young men who might have, in another time, been given grief counseling or been treated for posttraumatic stress disorder but instead were led by the twin pipers of Quantrill and Anderson, one intent on undeserved gain and glory, the other burning for dark revenge. Lawrence had been the home of Jim Lane, John Brown and Colonel Charles Jennison. Its warehouses were well stocked by them with goods and personal belongings that had been stolen at gunpoint from Missouri homes. Men from there had crossed into Missouri time after time to rob, kill and plunder Missouri's farms and towns. Regular public auctions dispersed these stolen goods into many of the homes of the townspeople—at bargain prices—marking their complicity in the work of the marauders. In the warped world in which Quantrill's men lived, the Lawrence massacre seemed a just and orderly act of war—little different from the Kansans' sack and destruction of Osceola (though the nine lives forfeited there pale in comparison to the price extracted from Lawrence).

The attack on Lawrence was painted at the time (and, in many quarters, since) as the most heinous action of the Civil War (Order Number 11, Sherman's March to the Sea and the Sand Creek Massacre notwithstanding). Lawrence, with a population of two thousand, was not defenseless at the time of the attack. It was simply poorly defended. There was a small military camp across the river from town. Quantrill's men were able to cut the unguarded lines to the ferry. Camped two hundred yards apart just south of the business district were men of the Second Kansas Colored Regiment and the Fourteenth Kansas Infantry Regiment, still asleep in their tents, with no guard on duty and their weapons stored a block away. The guerrillas rode through the camps knocking their tents down over them and shooting into the canvas, killing most of the men in the Fourteenth. Approaches to the town were left unguarded, and Federal forces, as well as militia units, had concentrated near the Missouri border. There were members of the home guard who were armed, but the guerrillas simply overwhelmed the town with the sudden, efficient and violent attack. The guerrillas were on their way back to Missouri long before noon.

The prison collapse in Kansas City and the personal loss of several of the guerrillas involved in the attack cannot be discounted as one motivation behind the destruction that was unleashed that day. Outraged (and likely embarrassed), General Thomas Ewing reacted only three days later by issuing the infamous General Order Number 11. This action effectively displaced twenty thousand people in four counties along the Missouri/Kansas border, with less than two weeks notice. All people living in rural areas of the four counties were to leave their homes, whether they were loyal or not. Those who could prove loyalty would be allowed to live in the region in communities near military posts. Those who could not were to leave the state, and their homes were burned to the ground. Once again, the innocent were punished with the guilty. To add insult to injury, Kansas troops under Jennison were allowed to help in the enforcement of the order. Martha Young, daughter of slaveholder Solomon Young (and later the mother of Harry S Truman), was forced to leave her home. Cole Younger's mother, Bursheba Fristoe Younger; Jesse James's mother, Zerelda James; and countless others, many of whom had formerly been part of the financial and cultural elite of their communities in western Missouri, were evicted. Many of the families living in the affected counties (Bates, Cass, Jackson and Vernon) moved into Westport or Kansas City, swelling the numbers of Confederate sympathizers in the towns.

Senator Lane felt that Order Number 11 didn't go far enough and threatened to cut an even broader swath of destruction in Missouri. On September 9, 1863, Lane gathered nearly one thousand Kansans at Paola and began marching toward Westport with the intent of destroying the pro-slavery town. Ewing sent several companies of the Kansas Eleventh to intervene. Lane finally backed down.

Order Number 11 had little effect on Confederate operations in Missouri. The guerrillas found plenty of forage in the abandoned fields and farms of the border counties, though many went south to Texas or Arkansas for the winter. The civilian population, few of whom directly supported the guerrillas, suffered the most, and the state was poorer for the loss of many farms and small communities and their produce. The guerrilla groups would return ahead of Price, doing some of their worst damage in Missouri in 1864.

By 1864, Missouri had given 40,000 men to the armies of the Confederacy and 110,000 to the Union. Casualties numbered in the tens of thousands. In Kansas, roughly two-thirds of men between the ages of eighteen and sixty had served, and nearly one-third of them became casualties. The economies of both states had suffered horribly. Great amounts of wealth had changed hands or been destroyed by the border raids.

Pro-slavery families had to sell off property to put up deposits to remain in their homes, many of which were later burned. The economy and society had been turned upside down in the course of a few years.

Kansas had an extended drought, and many settlers there simply gave up and moved west to greener pastures. Nearly thirty thousand settlers had left the state in response to the horrible conditions there prior to the war. Those who remained would suffer four years of hardship, tragedy and loss.

Some war-weary Kansans and Missourians picked up stakes and moved west to California or Colorado. Samuel Clemens (Mark Twain) left his militia unit and headed for the gold fields and peace. John Behan, who had a Southern mother and a Union father, opted to head west, ending up as sheriff of Cochise County, Arizona (where he was present for the shootout at the O.K. Corral).

Exact figures aren't available, but it appears that Westport and Kansas City both had significant decreases and changes in population. The number of businesses that existed before the war declined, and most changed ownership. Those who remained suffered much, and as the army tried to exert greater control, the guerrillas seemed to keep getting stronger. Many looked to the fall elections to change the tide of the war. Southerners hoped the radical Republicans and Lincoln would be ousted and peace might be achieved with a different administration.

In the summer of 1864, General Edmund Kirby Smith was in command of the trans-Mississippi for the Confederacy. The previous year's losses at Vicksburg, Mississippi, and Port Hudson, Louisiana, had split the eastern and western forces of the Confederacy. Union control of the Mississippi River prevented significant troop movement between the

General Edmund Kirby Smith sent Price on his ill-fated raid of Missouri. *Courtesy of the Library of Congress.*

two theaters. The South's two largest armies were under siege at Atlanta and Richmond, and a new plan of action was desperately needed.

A plan hatched by Confederate commissary Captain J. Henry Behan out of Mississippi had been floating around from Jefferson Davis to Braxton Bragg and back concerning a raid from the trans-Mississippi. The captain had boldly written a number of letters to Davis outlining his plan. Davis had passed it on to his secretary of war, James Seddon, and General Braxton Bragg, soliciting their opinions of its merits. Behan's plan was to create a new front in the West, invading from Arkansas up into Kentucky and on into Tennessee and cutting into Sherman's supply lines. The plan was impractical. The Union navy had too strong a hold on

Confederate president Jefferson Davis supported an invasion of Missouri. *Courtesy of the Library of Congress.*

the Mississippi for a crossing in force. Bragg still ordered Edmund Kirby Smith in August to send General Richard Taylor to attempt to move troops east of the Mississippi, but the plan was ultimately abandoned. Arkansas troops were resisting the orders, and Taylor saw no practical way to accomplish the crossing. Smith wrote to Davis outlining the reasons the crossing was untenable, but he held out the possibility of another plan—a raid into Missouri. Smith had not been able to deliver troops east of the Mississippi, but an invasion of Missouri would surely pull Union troops west of it.

The year 1864 had been a hard one for the Confederacy, and Ulysses S. Grant's ascendancy did not bode well for its future plans. Northern copperheads who opposed the war and hoped a peace could be worked out with the ouster of Lincoln and the radical Republicans conspired with Southerners to effect some sort of change that could turn public

General Ulysses S. Grant owned a slave, voted against Lincoln and was almost captured at Belmont, Missouri. *Courtesy of the Library of Congress.*

sentiment against the Union. Wild plans and conspiracies charged the imaginations of Southern idealists. The invasion of Missouri in many ways was more of a political operation than a military one. Confederate major general Sterling Price was convinced that if he entered Missouri with a large force, he would be able to rally thousands of Missouri men to his banner and retake control of the state. He even planned on bringing Lieutenant Governor Thomas C. Reynolds to be sworn in as governor (Governor Claiborne Jackson had passed away by this time). If he succeeded, it could cause a disruption of the national elections. Born of an optimism that is hard to imagine in hindsight, this raid was insufficient in terms of arms, men and supplies. General Edmund Kirby Smith could have easily sent infantry support and thousands more troops if he had been truly committed to the plan. Instead, Price's raid would be a desperate attempt at relevance in terms of the larger conflict, and yet it would have far-reaching consequences for the state and even the nation.

In 1863, there were draft riots in New York. The war was increasingly seen as a rich man's war and a poor man's fight, as the wealthy often were able to buy their way out of service. The Union had suffered horrible casualties, and each great battle brought word of more loss. Even the victories like Vicksburg and Gettysburg had come at the cost of tens of thousands of souls from the North. The loss of St. Louis, Jefferson City or, for that matter, any of several towns in Missouri or Kansas could help presidential candidate George McClellan's chances at unseating Lincoln and placing a man in the White House with whom the South might better hope to negotiate peace. Even if St. Louis and Jefferson City could not be won, a raid could bring cattle, horses and other desperately needed supplies, as well as new recruits from Missouri, to fill the decimated ranks of the Confederate armies.

Sterling Price had worked diligently from the early days of the war to gain access to potential supporters trapped north of the Missouri River. He had been stymied each time he had attempted to regain control of his home state. Finally, the Confederacy's level of desperation had hit the point where a conservative approach seemed hopeless. Daring plans, desperate raids (like that of Jubal Early in July 1864) and even covert action (like the Confederate attempt to burn down New York City, carried out only days after the Battle of Westport) were all on the table. While plots to kidnap or kill Abraham Lincoln were being advanced in the East, a long-shot military action that had a chance to bring men, arms and supplies to the ailing armies of the South was being given consideration in the West.

Courage Alone

Courage can win battles, but not alone. It took courage for Major General Sterling Price to lead his ragged army into Missouri in 1864. Lacking sufficient arms or numbers of men to complete their assigned mission, they sallied forth in relatively good spirits. The Missourians who had remained with Price must have looked forward to returning to their state as liberators. Their exile in Arkansas had been a source of great frustration. Price had carried his own frustrations with him since the First Battle of Lexington in 1861. Even after that victory, he had been forced to turn away several thousand volunteers he could have used but could not have fed or armed. In the years that followed that high-water mark, Price's forces had seen victory on ground he could not hold (in Missouri) and defeat on ground he did not want (in Arkansas, Mississippi and Louisiana).

In early 1864, Price had received communication from members of a secret pro-Confederate organization in Missouri called the Order of American Knights (OAK), which led him to believe that tens of thousands of Missouri men were just waiting behind Union lines and north of the Missouri River to aid his invasion. Price enthusiastically accepted the information as valid and passed it on to his superiors as reason to act. Price took his service to the state seriously, and though he was not a young man, he was still keen for another fight to regain the state he'd lost.

Price wrote to Lieutenant General Edmund Kirby Smith, commander of forces in the trans-Mississippi, on July 23, 1864, stating that he had been assured that the Confederate flag flew over "nearly all the principle towns of North Missouri" and that a move into the state could bring together a force of "not less than 30,000" for the Confederacy. General Kirby Smith commanded Price to move on Missouri. Price's orders were to make St. Louis his primary objective, but failing that he should retreat through Kansas and the Indian Territory and gather supplies, livestock and, most importantly, volunteers along the way. In August 1864, Price organized a cavalry force of twelve thousand men he called the Army of Missouri. He had fourteen artillery pieces, and though he needed more arms and ammunition, his cavalry was ready to do good service. The infantry troops that had been part of his original plan were reassigned shortly before the raid.

General Joseph O. Shelby was charged with covering Price's movement by attacking the railroad in northeast Arkansas. Shelby took six forts and several hundred prisoners and destroyed ten miles of track in the process. He also rounded up hundreds of recruits for the invasion, including many Confederate deserters whom he convinced to rejoin the cause at the point of a gun. On the other side of the state, General Stand Watie's Indian Brigade further occupied Federal forces with a feint toward southern Kansas. Price left Camden, Arkansas, on August 28, 1864, crossing the Arkansas River north of Little Rock. He made his way around Major General Frederick Steele's lines and then proceeded north to Pocahontas, Arkansas, where he joined Shelby, linking up with all the elements of his force.

Price put his army in order according to General Kirby Smith's orders, with one division under General Jo Shelby, consisting of Shelby's own "Iron Brigade" commanded by Colonel David Shanks; Tyler's brigade, under Colonel Charles H. Tyler; and another brigade commanded by Colonel Sidney Jackman. Shank's brigade was made up of veteran fighters from Missouri, each armed with several pistols and a carbine or rifle. Jackman's brigade consisted of some fifteen hundred mostly new recruits from Missouri, more than half of whom weren't armed. Tyler commanded Missouri cavalry units and some of Shelby's new recruits. Shelby's division was ably supported by a four-gun Parrott battery commanded by Captain Richard Collins. Colonel James F. Fagan commanded another division consisting of four brigades under Brigadier

General William L. Cabell, Colonel Archibald S. Dobbin, Colonel William F. Slemons and Colonel Thomas H. McCray. Cabell's brigade was the most battle ready and experienced of Fagan's division. General John S. Marmaduke commanded Price's third division, consisting of Marmaduke's brigade, commanded by Brigadier John B. Clark Jr., and Freeman's brigade, commanded by Colonel Thomas R. Freeman. Marmaduke's artillery consisted of two batteries of three guns each under Major Joseph H. Pratt. General Clark's brigade was made up of veteran fighters, but many had become ill, weakening the unit somewhat. Price stayed in Pocahontas preparing his army for four days, shoeing horses and mules, distributing ammunition and supplies and attending to other details. Marching in three parallel columns, with Fagan's division in the center, Shelby on the left and Marmaduke on the right, Price's Army of Missouri finally entered Missouri on September 19, 1864.

Waiting, in anticipation of Price's raid, was the Union commander of the Department of Missouri, General William S. Rosecrans. With only eleven thousand Federal troops at his disposal, Rosecrans had chosen not to concentrate at the Arkansas line even after word of Price's movement had come. His forces were spread out across the state pursuing guerrillas or protecting likely targets from them. If he concentrated his forces without knowing Price's intended target, he would risk widespread damage from the guerrillas and still might be skirted around by Price, just as Steele had been in guarding Little Rock. Rosecrans had requested and received forty-five hundred veteran infantry troops under General A.J. Smith (who had been en route to support General Sherman) to help defend the state. It wasn't until September 23 that Rosecrans finally got word that Price had evaded Steele and Shelby had joined him in northeast Arkansas. He began concentrating forces at Price's most likely targets of St. Louis, Jefferson City and Rolla. On September 24, Shelby's cavalry was reported to have been seen near Pilot Knob, about ninety miles south of St. Louis.

Price's three columns had spread out and taken parallel routes north, with twenty-mile intervals between them, foraging as they went. All three columns headed for a predetermined rendezvous point of Fredericktown, Missouri, from which they intended to proceed to St. Louis. Shelby arrived first, followed by Price and Fagan's division on September 24. Marmaduke arrived on the twenty-fifth.

Price was informed by spies that A.J. Smith's forces had concentrated south of St. Louis and that a garrison of fifteen hundred men was stationed at Pilot Knob. Shelby suggested bypassing Pilot Knob, but Marmaduke and Fagan encouraged Price not to leave the force there behind his lines. Price decided to attack Pilot Knob, perhaps hoping to supply arms for more of Shelby's recruits or to clear his path north. Price sent Shelby north to destroy part of the Iron Mountain Railroad in order to prevent Smith from aiding the troops at Pilot Knob. Fagan and Marmaduke headed toward Arcadia and Ironton, Missouri, passing through Shut-In Gap, but Federal forces (including some two hundred Iowa soldiers sent under General Thomas Ewing for a reconnaissance in force) gave them stiff resistance. A combination of nightfall, rain and the stout resistance of Smith's Iowa troops stopped the Confederate advance until morning.

At sunrise on the twenty-seventh, Fagan, with Marmaduke's support, began to advance again, driving back Union pickets through Arcadia, Ironton and Pilot Knob. The first real battle of the campaign at Fort Davidson (near Pilot Knob, Missouri) would be perhaps the most costly in terms of wasted time and resources and in damage to the overall plan's chances of success.

On September 27, 1864, Price's men had forced back the Union troops and were surrounding the fort. Fort Davidson had fourteen guns and a complement of around one thousand men. Brigadier General Thomas Ewing (brother-in-law of General William T. Sherman) had just recently arrived at the fort with two hundred Iowa soldiers (veterans of A.J. Smith's infantry) to augment the small force there. He had been scouting possible routes that Price might take to invade when he found out that the railroad between his troops and St. Louis had been cut by Confederate cavalry. Driven into the fort with a force of fewer than one thousand men, Ewing refused several demands to surrender, choosing to make a stand rather than place himself in the hands of the Missourians (who had no love for Ewing after his issue of the infamous Order Number 11). Ewing was outnumbered more than ten to one, but it was more than courage that drove him to fight on. Ewing had African American civilians inside the fort and was concerned, in the wake of the recent Fort Pillow massacre of African American troops, that surrender would not guarantee their safety

General Thomas Ewing successfully delayed Price at Pilot Knob and escaped to Rolla. *Courtesy of the Library of Congress.*

or, for that matter, his own. Price assembled troops on the surrounding hills and made several separate, uncoordinated charges at the fortified position. The fort was well designed with nine-foot-high and ten-foot-thick walls, a nine-foot-deep dry moat, two rifle pits extending out from the walls, cleared fields of fire for nine hundred feet all around and the only access limited to a single drawbridge on the southeast corner. In addition, the fort was equipped with four thirty-two-pounder siege guns, three twenty-four-pounder howitzers and three twelve-inch mortars, as well as six additional field guns.

Price had intended to bombard the fort from the two high points nearby, Shepherd Mountain and Pilot Knob, but had been informed—incorrectly—that Union forces had Confederate civilian hostages within the fort. Having been implored not to risk the civilians in a bombardment and told by Generals Fagan and Marmaduke that they could easily take the fort without the cannonade, Price tried to overwhelm the defenders with a massive attack from several sides. The attacks fell apart, though, as they became uncoordinated, and the green brigades in both Fagan's and Marmaduke's divisions collapsed under fire. Only Cabell's and Clark's divisions held together for the assault, but having arrived separately, they were both forced to retreat with heavy losses. Shelby was nearly twenty-five miles away, near Potosi, tearing up sections of the Iron Mountain Railroad tracks. Price had sent messages asking Shelby to return to help with the siege, particularly wanting Collin's battery in place, but Shelby did not receive the word in time. Price put his engineers to work that night building ladders to scale the walls of Fort Davidson, but his troops had no chance to use them.

On the night of the twenty-seventh, Ewing decided the post was untenable. He had lost a fourth of his command in two days' time, so he made preparations to escape. A large piece of canvas was placed on the drawbridge to muffle the sound of the retreating Federals. Slipping stealthily out at 3:00 a.m., Ewing left a slow fuse burning in the powder magazine; an hour later, there was a devastating explosion. Ewing found a break in the Confederate lines and boldly passed right through. Unaware of the cause of the explosion or of Ewing's retreat, the Confederates assumed there'd been an accident in the fort and hoped the Federals would surrender in the morning. It was 8:00 a.m. before Price realized what had happened and noon before a pursuit began. Shelby was at Potosi doing damage to the Iron Mountain Railroad and was not aware of the escaping Federals.

The defenders of Fort Davidson had escaped, and the arms and ammunition that Price's army so desperately needed were gone as well. The Army of Missouri had lost three days, fifteen hundred men and all chances of catching Union forces in St. Louis off guard. Price sent Marmaduke after Ewing and the defenders of Fort Davidson; the chase and escape were supreme adventures, but also blunders. Ewing had intended to retreat toward St. Louis, but at Caledonia (about ten miles north of Pilot Knob) he found out Shelby had taken Potosi and his way was blocked. He determined to head west toward Rolla over a narrow road that was flanked by steep cliffs. Shelby and Marmaduke linked up to pursue Ewing at Caledonia. Even though Ewing's force was on foot and had civilian refugees to slow their march, they were able to stay ahead of Marmaduke and Shelby, at least in part because of rearguard action by the Iowa troops and the battery preventing pursuit down the narrow lane. The pursuit continued through the twenty-eighth and into the evening of the twenty-ninth, when Ewing's exhausted force finally halted to make a stand, hoping that help would arrive from Rolla, some thirty-five miles away, before his command was overtaken. His troops set up breastworks made of rails and ties and waited for the Confederate attack. But by that point in the pursuit, Marmaduke had dropped out, and Shelby couldn't see the point of attacking a force that was in a fortified position that wasn't on the way to their target of St. Louis. Marmaduke concurred that capturing the force wasn't worth risking the losses it might inflict.

Ewing and the defenders of Fort Davidson made their way to Rolla. Price took Fagan's troops within forty miles of St. Louis and then lost his nerve, realizing he no longer had sufficient forces to move on the town, since they were off chasing Ewing. General Ewing and the defenders of Fort Davidson had inflicted heavy casualties, deprived Price's army of needed arms and equipment, delayed his advance by days (giving St. Louis more time to fortify its defenses), goaded Price into dividing his forces and escaped to Rolla and preserved the majority of his force. Word of their success spread quickly, and Ewing was eventually congratulated by President Lincoln in person for his actions. Price now turned toward Jefferson City, hoping to regain the seat of power from the appointee government.

To Union commanders in Missouri, the motives and goals behind Price's raid were still unknown. General William S. Rosecrans had hoped General Steele would keep Price bottled up in Arkansas, as demand for troops east of the Mississippi, as well as term of enlistment limits on volunteer forces, had reduced the number of Union troops available to him. Rumors of an invasion had surfaced in the spring, and

General William S. Rosecrans chased Price across the state, never quite catching up until Westport. *Courtesy of the Library of Congress.*

Rosecrans had raised some militia units in anticipation of a fall attack, but Missouri was a big piece of real estate to watch over. Guerrilla activity had spread troops out across the state, as protecting towns, railroads and supplies from the marauders kept thousands of troops engaged in the field. Clearly, the Federal authority had a sufficient numerical advantage in available troops to defeat Price's force, but not if it couldn't concentrate them in one place. The problem in 1864 was that communication and transportation were major challenges under the best of circumstances. There was only one railroad crossing the length of the state, the St. Joseph–Pacific, and it had been attacked and sabotaged so much that it was nearly closed down. Wires were cut, trains were derailed or burned and even riverboats were occasionally fired on or taken over.

Rosecrans had gathered some forces at Jefferson City but had concentrated his efforts on defending St. Louis. Price's army stretched out over five miles and was traveling at a pathetic pace of fifteen miles per day. While Union forces were busy fortifying the town, Price's command was fighting a losing battle to maintain discipline among the poorly armed, poorly trained and poorly motivated recruits who made up a significant portion of the force. Since Price's men had to forage for necessities on the march, there was little chance of preventing those who were inclined to do so from extracting any plunder they came across in the little towns and farms in their path. On October 6, General Shelby forced a crossing of the Moreau Creek six miles from the capital. In the skirmish, Colonel David Shanks was killed. Price replaced him with Brigadier General M. Jeff Thompson. The next morning, they took positions on the hills south of Jefferson City. Had Price traveled at a pace that wasn't slow for infantry, let alone a cavalry force, he would have found Jefferson City relatively undefended. The majority of the garrison and a battery of eight cannons didn't reach Jefferson City until the sixth. Arriving on October 7, Price deployed and presented as if he intended to attack but, after a short cannonade, withdrew his troops.

Price had become more cautious after Pilot Knob. When his spies (incorrectly) placed the number of Union troops in and around town at fifteen thousand, he determined to bypass it and head for Boonville and the river counties to recruit more men. The first two objectives of his mission were beyond his reach, and the general uprising in Missouri had failed to materialize. Rosecrans sent General A.J. Smith and his forty-five hundred experienced infantrymen after Price, but they could not keep up with the mounted invaders. Rosecrans needed more mobility, and in Jefferson City, newly arrived General Alfred Pleasonton was able to prepare it. Forming three cavalry brigades under Rosecrans's district commanders (Generals Sanborn, Brown and McNeil), Pleasonton put General John S. Sanborn in temporary command of the three brigades (approximately four thousand mounted men) and ordered them to pursue Price in order to observe, harass and delay his actions. Sanborn followed

Price, and on October 9, near Russellville, he engaged the rearguard under General Fagan. Price continued northwest toward the old river town of Boonville.

On October 10, townspeople in Boonville greeted Price and his army as liberators. Price recruited over 1,000 young men there. Guerrillas led by Lieutenant William "Bloody Bill" Anderson arrived in Boonville on October 10. William Anderson had earned the sobriquet "Bloody Bill" in part for the grisly carnival of destruction he had perpetrated in Centralia, Missouri, a railroad town founded in 1857. On September 27, 1864, while Price was attacking Pilot Knob, Anderson and his men looted the town; stopped and emptied a train there, set it on fire and sent it barreling down the tracks to the next town; killed, maimed and scalped 24 unarmed Union soldiers who had been on the train and robbed the rest of the passengers; and then set the depot on fire and rode out of town. A contingent of 155 men from the Thirty-ninth Missouri Infantry (mounted) pursued Anderson and his men, only to be outmaneuvered and routed. Anderson and his men rode down the inexperienced troopers, pursuing and killing the retreating men all the way back to Centralia. Anderson's men killed 123 of the 155 troopers and then mutilated the bodies, leaving a surreal display of jumbled body parts in the field. The scalps of his grisly victory were still hanging from his saddle as he went to meet General Price at Boonville. Price ordered the scalps removed before he would meet with Anderson, but he did meet with him and other guerrilla leaders, giving them orders and assigned objectives.

Also arriving near Boonville on the tenth were Union troops from Jefferson City led by General Sanborn. Generals Marmaduke and Fagan quickly repulsed the Union troops, who retreated below the Petit Saline River. Sanborn's men had been thirty-six hours without rations, so he retired to the town of California, Missouri, where he obtained four days' rations and gained an additional cavalry brigade of fifteen hundred men. By October 11, much of Boonville's wealth had been liberated in a two-day debauch that served to occupy Price's troops while he pondered his next steps. Sanborn returned to Boonville on October 13 to find that Price had already abandoned it and was moving west again.

By October 13, 1864, Price had sent troops north to Glasgow under Generals Shelby and John Bullock Clark Jr. and south to Sedalia under

General M. Jeff Thompson. It was believed that a considerable store of arms would be found in Glasgow. Attacking on October 15 at dawn, Confederate artillery drove the Union forces back to their fortifications. Union commander Colonel Chester Harding surrendered at 1:30 p.m. Though Union troops were able to destroy part of the supplies there, needed rifles, overcoats and horses were all obtained in Glasgow. Casualties were Union, four hundred, to Confederate, fifty. The supplies and victory gave a needed boost to the morale of Price's troops.

In Sedalia, Brigadier General M. Jeff Thompson, with troops from Shelby's Iron Brigade numbering about fifteen hundred men, attacked the town at the same time Shelby and Clark were attacking Glasgow. Union militia defending the town was quickly overwhelmed by Thompson's larger force. Thompson's men started to loot the town, but he pulled them back and told them to just take the arms and equipment they had obtained from the militia and return to Price's main force.

Back in Kansas, the border towns were filling with men. Seventeen thousand had reported for duty by Saturday, October 15, 1864. Troops from Colorado and western Kansas were rushed to the border. General James Blunt broke off from fighting Indians near Fort Larned and rode full out for Fort Leavenworth in response to Curtis's call for help. Kansas City was under martial law. Mayor Van Horn asked all the city's businesses to close at 4:00 p.m. and send all able-bodied men to drill at the courthouse. The situation was complicated by Order Number 11, as Westport and Kansas City had filled with Missourians who had been displaced by the order, many of whom would likely be happy to see Price and his men come for a visit. Colonel Jennison had taken over the Harris home for himself and occupied his troops in searching out and harassing anyone suspected of being disloyal.

Price again delayed until October 18, waiting at Waverly for his returning troops from Sedalia and Glasgow, his caravan moving at a snail's pace across the state. With hundreds of wagonloads of booty and a few thousand head of cattle, it must have looked like a scene from Exodus more than a military operation. Price had been ordered to gather needed supplies and recruits, but in gaining and transporting them, he lost precious time. Price advanced toward Lexington. Telegraph wires were cut east of Independence, leaving Westport and other border

General James G. Blunt led delaying actions against Price at Lexington, Little Blue and Byram's Ford. *Courtesy of the Library of Congress.*

towns deaf to the sound of approaching hoof beats. In the camps along the Kansas border, agents of Governor Thomas Carney had stirred contention, lampooning those who believed Price would come. Doubt was growing, and many hungry men sleeping in tents along the prairie near Westport were ready to believe this had all been a hoax. The Carney faction wanted these men back in their towns in time for the November election, not sitting in the camps along the border or, worse yet, off on some wild goose chase in Missouri.

Finally, word of Price's whereabouts arrived. The Carney faction had erred. Senator James Lane, who had taken to his sickbed, over anxious about his chances of reelection, heard the news. Lane was revived by the opportunity that Carney's mistake had given him. Heading for the camps and a chance to redeem himself as the protector of Kansas, he hit the stump, decrying the Carney faction for failing to protect the state. He argued for swift invasion of Missouri rather than a fight on Kansas soil. Lane joined Blunt and entered Missouri, stopping at Pleasant Hill to rest and then proceeding toward Warrensburg. When Blunt arrived at Holden, he was notified of the whereabouts of the other Union commands. A.J. Smith's infantry was at California, Missouri, and Sanborn's cavalry was dogging Price's rearguard northwest of Sedalia. Blunt determined to meet Price at Lexington, hoping to trap him between the three forces.

Major General James G. Blunt set out from Holden on October 17 to beat Price to Lexington and, if possible, hold it. Marching into and through the night, Blunt arrived in Lexington ahead of Price. He found a few guerrillas who had occupied the town and quickly disposed of them. Blunt immediately went to work, ordering townsmen (black and white) to help build up the defenses. Blunt sent advance troops out on the roads Price might take into town. The Dover road was defended by Captain H.E. Palmer and 250 men of the Eleventh Kansas Cavalry. The Warrensburg road was protected by Captain Louis F. Green and Company B of the Eleventh Kansas and Company A of the Sixteenth Kansas Cavalry. Blunt sent word to Curtis that he had occupied the town and asked for reinforcements, but he soon realized he would be alone in this fight.

Lead elements of Price's force made contact with Union pickets at 2:00 p.m. and drove them back to the main force. Price's attack came on the Warrensburg, Dover and Salt Creek roads. On the Salt Creek and Warrensburg roads, Price's troops started pouring into position. Outnumbered, the Union forces made a stand at first but were eventually pushed back into town. On the Dover road, Captain Palmer's force held out against a force of about five hundred, battling back and forth until 5:00 p.m., when the guns fell silent. Blunt's main force had been pushed through to the west side of town. Blunt knew he was outgunned and withdrew before Price could deploy his larger cannons. Blunt retreated down the Independence road with his main force, after he assigned Colonel Thomas Moonlight to cover his retreat. Moonlight made four stands that evening, making good use of his cannons in delaying the Confederate advance until nightfall. Blunt's force finally stopped along the Little Blue River about 2:00 a.m. on the twenty-first.

Lost Opportunities

Battle of the Little Blue

Lost opportunities are rarely found again. The story of the Battle of Westport and of Price's raid is one of many opportunities lost. On October 21, General Rosecrans had the opportunity to trap Price in the valley of the Little Blue River between Curtis's forces and those of General Alfred Pleasonton (who had assumed command of and reorganized the provisional cavalry into four brigades on the nineteenth at Dunksburg, Missouri). The Little Blue River feeds into the Missouri River about five miles east of Independence. Communication, coordination, Kansas politics and simple command structure problems kept Rosecrans's opportunity from being realized. A well-coordinated attack could have easily trapped Price in the broad valley of the Little Blue. General Blunt saw an opportunity to fight Price on good ground well east of the trailhead towns on the morning of the twentieth and sent word to General Curtis suggesting he come forward to make a stand there. Curtis declined and ordered Blunt to withdraw to Independence. Blunt left Colonel Thomas Moonlight with four mountain howitzers and four hundred men from the Eleventh Kansas behind at the Little Blue to once again cover his retreat. Blunt led the rest of his force to Independence but continued to press his case for making a stand at the Little Blue. Blunt was convinced that the river presented the best ground to stop the Rebel advance, but by that time General Curtis had already begun fortifying his position at the Big Blue.

Colonel Thomas Moonlight's Eleventh Kansas Cavalry delayed Price at the Little Blue River with only four hundred men. *Courtesy of the Library of Congress.*

Price was entering a broad valley, with the Missouri River to the north, Blunt to the west, Pleasonton to the east (he had moved the provisional cavalry to Lexington late on the night of the nineteenth) and infantry under A.J. Smith coming up from the south: a trap. General Curtis was convinced, however, that the Kansas volunteers would refuse orders to move so far into Missouri, and he lacked sufficient troops of his own to stop Price long enough for Rosecrans's forces to catch up. The political faction supporting Governor Carney feared that Senator Lane and the radical Republican candidates would benefit if the militiamen were stuck in Missouri and unable to vote. A campaign was organized by the Carney faction within the camps, encouraging the men not to cross into Missouri. Curtis and Lane were blasted as being alarmists. Consequently, many men in the camps on the border still doubted that Kansas was Price's target, and if it was, why should they leave it unprotected to go chasing him in Missouri? Curtis had hoped a few days earlier to move out in force to Lexington and meet Price there; he now had another opportunity to attack at the Little Blue River but simply could not take full advantage

View from the Union position on the Little Blue River. They faced west on good ground, with steep banks and thick brush. *Courtesy of Jay Rothman.*

of it. Blunt did convince Curtis to let him mount a delaying action at the Little Blue, but only with the forces at his disposal in Independence.

Moonlight and his men had established a wire connection to Independence and awaited news of relief, either from the west or the east. On the morning of the twenty-first, Curtis gave Blunt orders to return to the Little Blue with the rest of his force (plus nine hundred men and six more cannons he had obtained while in Independence). Hoping to delay Price until Pleasonton could arrive, Blunt arrived that morning to find Colonel Moonlight under attack, his forces driven back from the east and west banks of the river and the bridge burned. Blunt immediately joined the fight and attempted to regain the defensive positions he had originally held. But with fewer than three thousand men to Price's more than eight thousand, and with Pleasonton still at Lexington, his battle was all uphill, even though he held the higher ground.

The fight began at dawn before Blunt arrived. Colonel Moonlight had kept his men busy erecting obstacles at all the low-water crossings the day before, and rifles were trained on the most likely spots where a crossing

The wide valley of the Little Blue River from the east, where Curtis and Rosecrans missed an opportunity to trap Price. *Courtesy of Jay Rothman.*

could be attempted. The Little Blue was shallow, and there were potential crossings all along it. Moonlight's little force could only hope to delay the inevitable, holding onto the bridge and high ground so as to inflict the most damage possible. His two cannons were positioned to cover the bridge. Major Martin Anderson and two companies of men were placed on the east bank in front of and around the bridge to make approaching it expensive for Price's troops. Moonlight and his men from the Eleventh Kansas had spent an entire day preparing for Price's attack, not knowing if they would be reinforced or when the army that outnumbered them more than twenty to one would arrive. He sent Captain Greer with Company I two miles downstream (north) to guard Blue Mills Crossing, and Captain Huntoon with Company H was stationed at another ford several miles away. Pickets fanned out east of the river for about a mile and waited.

On the morning of October 21, the lead elements of Price's force under General Marmaduke were on the move before first light. General Clark's brigade took the lead with Company D of the Fifth Missouri Cavalry under Captain D.R. Stallard in front as skirmishers. Around sunup, they encountered Anderson's pickets in the woods about a mile east of the bridge. Stallard's men dismounted and started to advance when a hail of fire belched out from behind the trees, killing or wounding a third of the company. The rest of Stallard's men surged forward, but the fire from the woods continued, hitting the horse holders and adding wounded and panicked horses to the mêlée on the field. The rush to the woods revealed that the Union skirmishers were unsupported, and they quickly turned and ran for the bridge. Colonel Moonlight telegraphed Blunt at Independence to inform him that he had engaged the enemy, was retreating and was in need of support. Curtis had finally agreed to let Blunt at least try to delay Price's advance at the Little Blue. Blunt added to his force at Independence another nine hundred men and six more cannons. When they received word of Moonlight's situation, Blunt's command quickly mounted their horses and galloped out of Independence toward the battlefield.

As Major Anderson's men regrouped to defend the bridge, Colonel Robert R. Lawther's Tenth Missouri Confederate Cavalry and Colonel Colton Greene's Third Missouri Cavalry rushed up behind Stallard and started down the slope toward the east bank of the river. Fire from Union sharpshooters on the west bank forced them to dismount and seek cover. Crowding Anderson's men in toward the bridge, the Confederates advanced slowly through a hail of fire from both riverbanks and the bridge. Marmaduke's forces kept advancing steadily, with Shelby's brigade in line to fill in behind them. The main prize was the bridge, as crossing the river with artillery and wagons would be much easier for Price if it was captured intact. Though Moonlight's men were well armed and well positioned, the weight of numbers was taking its toll. As the Confederates pushed forward, Major Anderson sent for a wagon (loaded with hay the night before) and set it ablaze to block the Confederates' progress and burn down the bridge. General Clark came up at this point and sent Lawther's Tenth Cavalry downstream (north) to take the ford below the bridge and Lieutenant Colonel Preston, with the Fourth Missouri Confederate Cavalry, to take the ford above it. He also sent Captain Stallard to see if the fire on the bridge could be stopped. The movement forced Moonlight's men to spread out to keep from being flanked and made it possible for Stallard to get several pieces of artillery across the bridge before it collapsed (the dry timbers were engulfed by the flames from the lit wagon).

There were stone walls, timber and lots of cover for over half a mile uphill from the west bank of the Little Blue, and Moonlight's tiny force made good use of the cover, contesting every inch of ground as they retreated up the banks and into the low hills behind them. A murderous fire from the four mountain howitzers kept the advancing cavalry from overwhelming Moonlight's dismounted force as it backed up the bluegrass-covered hills. Preston and Lawther had forced their way across the fords above and below the bridge, and Clark sent the remainder of his brigade across the river. Colonel Freeman's brigade filled in close behind Clark. The Confederates were now spreading out their attack, forcing Moonlight's men to also spread out ever thinner to avoid being flanked. Marmaduke's cavalry had crossed the river, and Shelby's force was dismounted and preparing to come across as well. Moonlight's men were low on ammunition and desperately outnumbered, but they held doggedly together, making the Confederates earn the ground they were taking. By 9:00 a.m., Companies I and H had returned to join the rest of Moonlight's force as it reached the heights of the hills overlooking the Little Blue. The tiny force was facing an army that outnumbered it at least twenty to one and presently threatened to engulf it by sheer

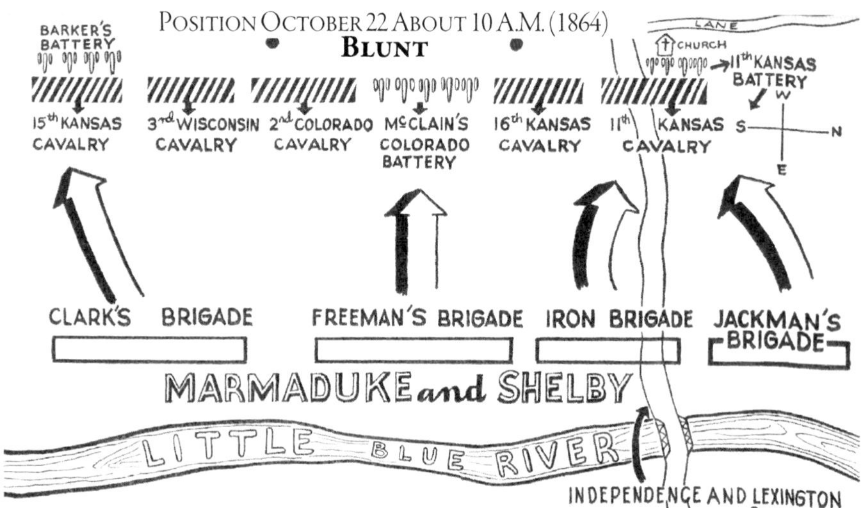

Map of the Battle of the Little Blue River showing the disposition of troops late on the morning of October 22, 1864. *Courtesy of the Westport Historical Society.*

weight of numbers. It was at this opportune moment that General Blunt arrived.

Blunt's force included the Sixteenth Kansas Cavalry, which he placed to the right of Moonlight's Eleventh, which in turn became the far left of the Union line. In the center he placed W.D. McClain's Independent Colorado Battery (with six rifled field pieces), and to McClain's right he placed Major J. Nelson Smith's Second Colorado Cavalry, followed by the Third Wisconsin Cavalry, with the Fifteenth Kansas Cavalry taking up the far right (with Lieutenant H.L. Barker's battery of five mountain howitzers supporting them). His troops formed ranks quickly, as Blunt had them dismount and send horses to the rear with every fourth man. The Confederates were dismounted as well, and when Blunt's troops came forward, hundreds of Rebels rushed up to meet them with a high-pitched yell. The Union attack began with McClain's battery pounding the Confederate center. As batteries on both sides joined in, the smoke sank low across the field and served as a screen on which the fire reflected and through which a macabre dance of mutilated men and horses writhed and ran mad. Men and horses fell together; one cavalryman with a broken leg and a bullet-shattered arm lay helpless as a large wounded horse trying to regain its feet tore his clothes apart with repeated blows from the calks (protrusions at the toe and heel that give the shoe a better grip) of its shoes. The battle line seesawed back and forth at first, as Blunt blunted the Confederates' numerical superiority with his better position and fresher forces. Rifle fire poured into both lines, as shrieking horses and screaming men absorbed the fire. Slowly, Blunt's forces drove the Confederates back, keeping up a steady cannonade. Finally, crawling on their stomachs, they closed and poured rifle fire into the smoke that marked the Rebel line, driving the center back nearly half a mile.

Marmaduke's division had filled the center and fanned out on the west bank of the river, and Shelby was crossing in force and filling in on Marmaduke's right. The Confederate force was spreading out with Clark's brigade on the left, Freeman's brigade in the center, Shelby's Iron Brigade stretching right of center and across the Independence road and Jackman's brigade on the far right. The Confederates once again threatened to flank Blunt, forcing him as they had Moonlight to retreat to the heights overlooking the river. At this point, General Curtis and his staff arrived from Independence. Curtis shifted the position of McClain's battery, ordering two of the cannons moved into a newly plowed field, leaving Blunt's left unprotected and the artillerymen exposed to Rebel sharpshooters. Major R.H. Hunt, chief of Curtis's artillery, then ordered two howitzers of the Eleventh Kansas Cavalry to join McClain's battery in support. The placement of the guns strengthened the center, and when the cannons opened on the Confederates with canister and spherical case (types of cannon ammunition that explode packed shot and shrapnel into enemy lines), the gray lines faltered and were driven back. Curtis's move of the cannons eventually proved disastrous, as Shelby's experienced troops quickly took advantage of the situation and surged against the Union left. Jackman's cavalry was sent forward under Lieutenant Colonel C.H. Nichols. Colonel Moonlight's unsupported brigade was forced to retreat against the onslaught. The exposed battery was now threatened by Shelby's advancing troops. Moonlight's battle-weary force turned once more to the aid of the battery, re-forming and attacking the Rebel right near the battery. They were supported by the quick action of Major J. Nelson Smith's Second Colorado Cavalry (most of whom rode white horses), who came galloping in, yelling and crashing into Shelby's advancing line. Major Smith was killed by a bullet through the heart as he led the gallant charge to save the battery. Sabers clashed and pistols cracked with sudden intensity as the horses and men swirled in close battle. Separating, the cannons had been saved and were moved to the rear as the remaining men of the Eleventh Kansas and Second Colorado covered the retreat.

Curtis had seen enough. Price would not be held at the Little Blue. He returned to Independence to evacuate his staff and move behind his fortifications at the Big Blue crossing. Blunt was finally forced to retreat toward Independence. He dismounted and divided his force into two units, and while one fought, the other retreated to a new defensive position and then they would trade turns. Time and again, they would delay the Rebels and then retreat to a new position. Blunt formed his men once more on the eastern edge of town, but the Rebel pursuit had abated, and by 5:00 p.m. Blunt decided to withdraw to Curtis's line at the Big Blue, leaving Colonel Walker and the Kansas Sixteenth Cavalry to defend the town. Blunt led the rest of his tired troops out of Independence, ordering the Sixteenth to hold its position until the Eleventh Kansas could resupply with ammunition and return to relieve it.

General Shelby had taken over the advance of Price's force and, realizing Blunt had withdrawn most of his force from town, pressed forward. Colonel Walker and the Sixteenth Kansas Cavalry were nearly out of ammunition when Colonel Moonlight's Eleventh Kansas returned to town to relieve them. Moonlight started one of his howitzers booming into the Rebel line, but the town was soon filled with men and horses coming down every street. The fighting became close and heated, spreading through the streets and alleys. The shops that had outfitted thousands of pioneers were riddled with bullets, breaking windows, knocking down canopy posts and spattering blood in the desperate fight. The main roads coming into town from the north and east were filled with combatants.

On Main Street was the Jackson County Jail (built in 1859 along with the marshal's home; the connected buildings are now a popular Independence museum). It had been used as a provost marshal's office,

Jail cells at the Independence 1859 Jail. Confederate prisoners were liberated on October 22, 1864. *Courtesy of the Jackson County Historical Society. Gift of Nick Vedros.*

and at the time of the raid it held several pro-Confederate prisoners who had been stuffed into its stone cells under Orders Number 10 and 11. This jail had held William Quantrill at one point, and several of the guerrilla fighters knew it well. It was the center of intense fighting. Once taken, the jailor was killed and the prisoners scattered with glee.

Union troops tried to make another stand near the old courthouse (started in the 1830s and still in use) on Liberty Street, where wagon trains once lined up for miles. The battle raged on, pushing through to the outskirts of town. Another stand was made at the railroad bridge. Finally, as darkness enveloped the town, Moonlight and his weary men retreated to the Big Blue River, reaching the Union lines near midnight.

The Battle of the Little Blue had merged into the Second Battle of Independence as the day wore on and would ultimately be considered the first day of the Battle of Westport. By nightfall, the town had seen its second Confederate victory of the war, but just like the first, this one would be short-lived.

General Curtis had evacuated his headquarters in Independence and effectively left the town to Price. In *The Rebel Invasion of Missouri and Kansas*, Richard Josiah Hinton wrote of the retreat: "The citizens of Independence appeared on the streets to scoff at our retiring troops and welcome their congenial traitors." Blunt had retreated to the Blue River, joining Curtis's line of defenses there. Price's troops camped near a railroad cut just west of Independence, the rearguard stationed at the edge of town.

No official tally of the lives lost at the Little Blue River has been made, though a pair of modest markers tells the story. No walking tour of the battlefield is prepared, and a highway runs through the middle of the battle line. No archaeological survey exists to tell what Price's train of wagons and the more than ten thousand combatants left behind in the river or on the farmland that now is threatened by encroaching development. A small park sits silent near one crossing, where cannons and rifles rang out and an opportunity was lost. An opportunity to preserve and promote the site of this battle still remains at the moment, but opportunities are fading fast.

Crossing the Blue

Crossing the Blue River had always been a difficult proposition. Westport had eclipsed Independence in part because it saved westward travelers that difficult crossing. For Price's army on October 22, 1864, crossing the Blue River (running south to north just east of the state line) appeared to be a hard task. General Curtis had sent Colonel Charles Blair and the Third Brigade to assist the engineers, who had kept busy building breastworks, rifle pits and other obstructions to passage in a tangle along the Blue River. The east bank of the Big Blue was less steep and had less vegetation than the west bank. To the west, the steep banks led up to a plateau that gradually rose from the river. At Byram's Ford, sharpened trees were in place on the high banks to impale Confederates trying to force a crossing. Troops were stationed from the mouth of the Blue at the Missouri River south to Hickman Mills.

Reinforcing the natural line of defense that the Blue River presented, Curtis hoped to stop Price's advance toward the city but had doubts of holding him with so much of his command being made up of untested Kansas volunteers. Curtis attempted to send a message to General Pleasonton through the Confederate lines, urging him to close in behind Price. A scout with the Second Kansas State Militia, Daniel W. Boutwell, set out at 7:00 p.m. on October 21 to contact General Pleasonton, carrying no arms or papers, only General George Deitzler's verbal instructions. Boutwell rode a horse to Kansas City, took a skiff down the Missouri, got the skiff caught on a bar in the river, abandoned the skiff, swam ashore, ran through the woods (skirting the Confederates at Independence), was fired at and narrowly missed, tried to cross a small stream on some fence rails but fell off into thick mud, managed to make it past the Confederate rearguard and then, just after daylight, reached General Pleasonton's pickets. Boutwell, covered in mud, was led to the general's tent and delivered Deitzler's message. Pleasonton determined to move immediately toward Independence.

Price moved out from the outskirts of Independence early on the twenty-second, sending Shelby to scout for a place to cross the Blue. General Curtis, after leaving Independence, set up headquarters on the Independence–Kansas City road behind a line that followed the Blue River from its mouth at the Missouri River south to Russell's Ford. His left, extending from the Missouri River to the main ford of the Blue, was placed under General Deitzler. His right, extending south from the main ford to Russell's Ford, was put under General Blunt. Blunt had argued with Curtis unsuccessfully the night before that Price would not ride straight down the main road to force a crossing; rather, he would feint and go farther upstream. Curtis was not moved, so Blunt dutifully distributed his forces on the west bank of the Blue, concentrating on Simmon's Ford (two miles south of the main ford) and Byram's Ford (five miles south of the main crossing). Shelby sent Colonel Jackman's brigade toward the main crossing so as to drive Curtis's pickets back and feint attack at the fortified ford. General Curtis had Colonel Ford send a battalion forward to meet Jackman's feint, but Jackman was not making a vigorous attack.

Curtis realized, too late, that Price's main attack would not come at the main crossing. There were only a few crossings on the Blue where the grade was not too steep, the water was shallow enough and the trail through the brush was wide enough for Price to get his wagons through. Shelby had to try and find a weakness in the defenses of one of them, but it would not be an easy task. Byram's Ford was a good crossing. General Blunt had placed Colonel McCain and a mounted battalion of the Fourth Kansas State Militia at Byram's Ford, and they were joined early Saturday morning by Colonel Jennison and the First Brigade (Jennison then taking command). Felled trees, sharpened with the points facing the river crossing, lined the ridge along the west bank

Mountain howitzers. Short-barreled, lighter-weight, maneuverable cannons fired canister rounds to devastating effect. *Courtesy of the Library of Congress.*

of the Blue. Sharpshooters waited behind trees and rock fences on the high ground west of the river. The south fork of the Independence road crossed Byram's Ford and led up a steep incline into the waiting mouths of five howitzers of Lieutenant H.L. Barker's battery. Behind Barker's guns waited Kansas State Militia units, the Fifteenth Kansas Cavalry and the Third Wisconsin Cavalry.

About 10:00 a.m., Colonel Jackman, who by this time had broken off his feint at the main ford and rejoined Shelby, dismounted part of his brigade and attempted a frontal assault on Jennison's forces at Byram's Ford. Supported by M. Jeff Thompson, Jackman repeatedly tried to force a crossing, only to be turned back by McCain's artillery. At 2:00 p.m., General Shelby, concerned that a crossing could not be forced at Byram's

Ford, sent Colonel Frank B. Gordon and the Fifth Missouri Confederate Cavalry upstream to find a crossing and Lieutenant Colonel Alonzo Slayback's Missouri Confederate Cavalry Battalion downstream to look for one. Slayback quickly came upon the unprotected and little-used Hinkle's Ford, pouring his troops across and into Jennison's left flank. Realizing too late what was happening, Blunt sent Colonel Moonlight and the Eleventh to support Jennison at Byram's Ford. Moonlight found his way blocked by Slayback's forces storming across the river and ended up racing Jennison to the state line south of Westport in order to stop the Rebel advance from continuing into Kansas. Farther south, Colonel Gordon also found a crossing between Jennison and General M.S. Grant's Kansas militia troops. Grant was at the far right of the Union line and had made the mistake of spreading his troops out, searching for the Rebel attack. He was therefore in no position to help Jennison when his line was pushed back. He took the forces he had at the Hickman Mills crossing and pulled back to the Mockbee Farm near the Harrisonville road in an effort to reunite with Jennison's line.

It was at the Mockbee Farm that some of the most intense fighting of the day took place. Colonel Gordon, reinforced by Jackman with a regiment and a battalion of cavalry, hit Grant hard. Grant formed his line in front of Captain Ross Burnes's old twenty-four-pound brass howitzer. Stubbornly holding their ground against the larger force, Grant's line was pushed back and re-formed twice, their cannons knocking holes in the Rebel attack. Finally at the edge of Mockbee's orchard, the Confederates had had enough of this little force. Gathering all their forces for a charge, the Rebels started their high-pitched yell. Grant's troops gathered in tightly behind Burnes, his twenty artillerymen and the old howitzer. The Rebel yell broke off as the charge commenced; the thunder of hoof beats shook the ground. In a matter of minutes, Grant no longer had a command. One hundred of his men were dead, including Burnes and all of his artillerymen; more were wounded, and 102 were taken prisoner.

Shelby's cavalry pushed Jennison back toward the state line, but Jennison resisted stubbornly, and when Moonlight fell in to support him, they began pushing M. Jeff Thompson's cavalry back. It was nearing dark as Thompson's forces withdrew to some wooded shelter. Shelby's forces had swept the high ground along the ridge, turning Blunt's flank

Battle of Byram's Ford. Price's forces flanked Union defenders here on October 22, 1864, forcing them back to Westport. *Courtesy of the Westport Historical Society.*

and forcing them back to Westport. They had gained the carefully laid-out defenses on the west bank of the Blue River (to be used against Pleasonton the next day), turned Curtis's right and forced his line back into Westport. Curtis ordered the Kansas militia units of George Deitzler into Kansas City, not knowing if they would be needed the next day to hold the town. Shelby had opened the crossing to the rest of Price's army. The wagons and cattle crossed and were sent down the road to the new Santa Fe, with Cabell's brigade as guard, while Price gathered his forces to face the army to his north.

Meanwhile, in Independence on the morning of the twenty-second, Pleasonton had finally caught up. He had a bridge constructed to replace the one Moonlight had burned and crossed the Little Blue. General John McNeil sent the Thirteenth Missouri Union Cavalry and the Seventeenth Illinois Cavalry forward as advance. They quickly engaged Price's rearguard, battering two of Fagan's brigades under Cabell and Slemons. Slemons's brigade took the brunt of the early fighting, as

Cabell's brigade had hurriedly moved the cattle and wagon trains through Independence toward Little Santa Fe. Captain W.M. Hughey's Arkansas Battery of Parrott guns supported Slemons's skirmishers, but McNeil's troops pressed forward. Fagan's troops had retreated from one position to another but had slowed McNeil's advance. Cabell's brigade came forward, and McNeil's troops slowed at the east edge of town. General Sanborn's Third Brigade was brought up, along with the Seventh Kansas Cavalry. It was nearing 3:00 p.m., and Pleasonton's forces were gathering to force their way into town. The people of Independence had hardly had time to catch their breaths from one day's fight before they were in the middle of the next.

General McNeil massed his cavalry to the east and northeast of town, ordering his mounted troops forward, sabers drawn, along the east edge of town. To the northeast of town, in what was supposed to be a coordinated attack, was General John Sanborn with the Second Arkansas Union Cavalry under the command of Colonel John E. Phelps. The advance of the far Union right got out in front of the general charge and pushed the gray line back into town. Entering town, Colonel Phelps had his troopers dismount and prepare for hand-to-hand combat in the streets—they didn't have to wait long. General Cabell and his Confederate Arkansas troops had come up to help Colonel Slemons, and the two groups of Arkansans slammed into each other in the streets of Independence. The mêlée that followed was tough and personal. The Union Arkansans captured three hundred of the Confederate Arkansans, and General Cabell himself barely avoided being taken.

Entering Independence from the east side, Colonel Edwin C. Catherwood with the Thirteenth Missouri Cavalry, supported by the Seventh Kansas under Major Francis Malone and the Seventeenth Illinois under Lieutenant Colonel John Lourie Beveridge, charged through town, driving Price's rearguard under Fagan before them. One group of Rebels tried to slow the advance at the Mormon temple lot and was nearly wiped out, with only a few survivors escaping. The charging cavalrymen pushed through town, capturing two brass six-pound cannons, complete with horses and drivers, and taking several Confederate soldiers prisoner.

The battle was witnessed from the second story of the Bingham-Waggoner Home by Mrs. Robert Hill. Mrs. Hill, in a letter to her sister,

Mrs. Kate Doneghy, gave her account of the events of the twenty-second and twenty-third. It reads in part:

> *I have braved a storm that is beyond all description. For the past two weeks the Federals have been massing all the forces they could on the border to capture Price and his army. It is estimated they had some 15,000 or 20,000 men. Ten thousand Kansas militiamen have been in camp here since Monday, also a regiment of Colorado troops. Three thousand of the militia-men were camped about our lot from Monday until Friday evening, when they were ordered out to meet the Rebels, as they called them.*
>
> *The fighting commenced about 9 o'clock in the morning, 6 miles from town, on the Lexington Road. The Confederates were laboring under a great disadvantage as the Federals had picked their ground and were entrenched behind rock fences. The Confederates had to charge all these fences. It would be impossible for me to tell you how many were killed and wounded but I understand that in this engagement the Federal's loss was greater than that of the Rebels. George Todd, the famous guerrilla, was mortally wounded in one of the charges, and died in town. Major Smith, a brave and courteous Federal officer who had command of the post here for the past eight months, was killed. A great many other officers met a similar fate in the desperate fighting near town.*
>
> *General Curtis gradually fell back until about 5 o'clock in the evening. Then the Confederates entered Independence, and for a time the fighting ceased. The Federals retreated to the Blue, the Confederates passing out as far as Rock Creek, where they rested a while and then took up their march to meet the enemy. At midnight we heard sharp firing right in front of town. Price's rearguard was stretched across the country for 6 miles. General Pleasanton attacked it in the morning with 10,000 cavalry. The fighting lasted all day, the roaring of the cannon and the clash of small arms was terrific. I am told that the list of the dead and wounded is distressingly large.*
>
> *The Confederates began to retreat about 3 o'clock, fighting desperately every foot of the way. They passed through town again firing with small arms at the oncoming Federals. The latter pushed so closely that at times they were not farther than 90 yards behind the Confederates.*

From the balcony in front of our house, which is very high, we had a clear view of the battle for more than a mile. We saw the Federals capture a battery in Noah Miller's field. It was magnificently defended, and no less bravely attacked. We could see the far-off flash of red fire coming out of the guns and pistols and men fell by the dozens. It was one of the most sublimely thrilling sights that no one could imagine.

From there on the Blue the fighting was fierce. The opposing forces were so close together that they used small arms almost exclusively, until they got to the Blue, when the cannonading commenced again. The guns would be wheeled into line with incredible swiftness and almost before you could count, the grape and canister would be seeping into the face of the charging legions. It seemed like the fighting extended all around us. The smoke rose high and almost darkened the sky.

The fighting ended about dark and was resumed again this morning [the twenty-third] *at about 7 o'clock in the neighborhood of Westport.*

Bingham-Waggoner Home. *Courtesy of the Jackson County Historical Society. Gift of Bingham-Waggoner Historical Society.*

> *It seems that General Price was only making a raid into Missouri, but some of the Southerners were hopeful that he would succeed. This evening a report comes that he is crossing the Kaw River and that he has suffered terribly, but as to this we do not know for certain. What happened here about Independence is all we know. There is a great deal of confusion. The dead and wounded are being carefully attended to today. The Jones Hotel is being used as the Confederate hospital, while the wounded are being taken to the Bank.*

Upon driving the Confederate rearguard to the west end of town, Generals Sanborn and McNeil were held back to secure the town, bring up the Federal wagon train and take care of the dead and wounded. General Pleasonton ordered the First and Fourth Brigades to take over the pursuit of Price's retiring rearguard. General Egbert Brown and his First Brigade took over the pursuit down the Independence/Westport road, driving the Rebels two miles farther from town. Running low on ammunition, Brown turned over the pursuit to Colonel Edward F. Winslow and his Fourth Brigade. Following the Rebels down the Byram's Ford road, the Fourth Brigade ran into Rebel pickets after dark. Colonel Edward F. Winslow deployed the Third Iowa Cavalry across the road, with the Fourth Iowa Cavalry and the Seventh Indiana Cavalry mounted in columns of four behind it. Winslow sent Colonel Frederick W. Benteen to the left to probe for the Rebel right. When Benteen engaged with the Rebel right, the sound of small-arms fire signaled the advance of the Third Iowa Cavalry. The Confederate rearguard had taken position along a small creek. Now under pressure from Winslow's force, they retreated again, and then again. By 10:30 p.m., Winslow had pushed them to within a few miles of Byram's Ford. From the darkness, a steady fire began to strike the Union advance, this from the Eighth Missouri Confederate Cavalry under Colonel William Jeffers of General Clark's brigade of Marmaduke's division. Winslow's troops were ordered to halt at this point and wait for a couple of hours for moonrise. With the advance halted, General Marmaduke determined to withdraw the remainder of his forces across Byram's Ford to the strong positions that had been taken from Colonel Jennison earlier in the day.

Price's army had been advancing for days, with little knowledge of the size of the forces arrayed against it in Westport and only recently learning of the size and proximity of Pleasonton's force. Price and Shelby were still hopeful that they could take Kansas City and then Leavenworth in the coming days. On the morning of the twenty-third, they would be disprized of all such notions. General Pleasonton's troops were gathered on the east bank of the Blue River, and Curtis, Blunt and Deitzler and the thousands of Kansas volunteers lined up south of Westport and along the state line, with Price's army in the middle. Price had already sent his wagon train south and had refused advice to retreat south with it. General Shelby convinced "old pap" that taking Westport and Kansas City was worth the risk. Forming ranks south of Westport, Price intended to engage Curtis's force, which included a large number of untried volunteers, hoping to defeat them while Marmaduke held Pleasonton at the Blue. Marmaduke had high ground and sharpshooters in place, as well as cannons loaded with shot; it would not be an easy crossing.

With Price on the west side of the Blue, Curtis was preparing to move his headquarters to safer ground. He had begun to withdraw his regular army troops to Wyandotte and even Leavenworth, but his subordinates from Kansas were furious at the idea, coming to Blunt with the suggestion that Curtis be removed from command. General Blunt tried no such action, but he persuaded Curtis to remain and fight. Those in favor of making a stand on both sides prevailed as the rasher, younger elements in both armies convinced the elder. But on the morning of October 23, luck had run out for the Confederates. Crossing a freezing cold river under fire from sharpshooters stationed behind cover on a hill overlooking one's position is never a great way to start the morning. General Pleasonton was not in the mood to hear complaints, though. His orders were to attack, as were Blunt's. This battle was to be fast and furious. Pleasonton's troops had come far in their pursuit of Price, and they were going to cross the Blue River come hell or high water. Before the day was over, they got a taste of both.

The Great Battle

Great battles can be fought even without the benefit of grand strategy; the action and actors themselves can accomplish the task. The Battle of Westport was a great battle. The commanders on each side (Price and Curtis) were both reluctant participants and would hardly top most historians' lists of great generals of the Civil War. Troops on both sides (including Kansas volunteers and much of Price's army) were labeled by various observers as motley, untrained, lacking in discipline—akin to criminals in their behavior. There were many veteran troops at Westport, some who had served on both sides of the Mississippi and to whom, by this date, death and destruction were old companions. However, a large number of the combatants were inexperienced volunteers and new recruits who would see their first, and in many cases their last, battle that day. What made the battle great was not the caliber of all the troops (though many were outstanding) or the generals (though some were exceptional); rather, it was the totality of the location, the stakes, the participants and the importance placed on the outcome by those involved and those watching from afar. This battle was intense, personal and desperate.

The Kansas and Missouri troops were fighting for their homes, their lives and their families. Price's wild gamble had reached its conclusion. His bet was called, and it seemed like all the chips were in and it was time to show cards. There would be no dignified meeting of generals as at

General Samuel R. Curtis, commander of the Department of Kansas and Indian Territory, led Union forces at Westport. *Courtesy of the Library of Congress.*

Appomattox. The war on the frontier could only end as it began, in fire and blood and desperation, with half-starved, exhausted and wounded men quitting the fight after there was no more left to give. More than men died here. The Civil War west of the Mississippi essentially would meet its end here, with Westport being the last and largest major battle in the West. The guerrilla uprising in Missouri would soon be broken, with the deaths of Todd at Independence and Bloody Bill at Richmond and Quantrill leaving the state, never to return alive. Kansas and Missouri would stay in the Union (officially) and cast their votes for the party of Lincoln. Just as armed conflict in the West over slavery and state sovereignty had augured the coming war in the East, the outcome of this great final battle in the West would presage the outcome of the greater conflict in the East.

The morning of October 23, 1864, was cold. Thousands of bone-tired, hungry men from both armies had collapsed in the fields and camps near Westport the night before. They woke up to a frosty, dreary Sunday morning, knowing this Sabbath day would be anything but a day of rest. General Curtis started the twenty-third at his headquarters in the Gillis House in Kansas City, perhaps regretting his decision to try and save the town rather than move across the state line to Wyandotte or farther upriver to Leavenworth. The die was cast before sunrise, though. Curtis had sent a message to Pleasonton stating his intention to throw all the Federal troops available into battle at dawn. Price also planned to attack in the morning, making his headquarters at the old "Boston" Adams House. He had placed Marmaduke in a strong defensive position to hold Pleasonton while he sent Shelby forward toward Brush Creek. Shelby was on good high ground south of Brush Creek, but with Curtis in his line of attack, Kansas volunteers to his left and Pleasonton massing on his right, he had only one narrow route of escape (south) if his attack failed. He would depend, as he so often had, on the Iron Brigade to take the lead. Shelby had argued in favor of attack, and he had time and again shown the ability to find a way through or around the enemy's defenses. Marmaduke had fended off first Sanborn and then Pleasonton in the trek across the state, and once again he was placed between Pleasonton and Shelby's right flank. Entrenched behind Union-built defenses captured the day before, the troops there were in good position to make crossing the Blue River unpleasant for Pleasonton.

Still, Price feared for his wagon train, which had swollen to six hundred wagons loaded with goods acquired in the raid, and his cattle herd, which numbered some three thousand head. Under the guard of only a brigade of General Cabell's command and a brigade of unarmed recruits under Colonel Charles H. Tyler, the wagon train and cattle herd were sent south past Little Santa Fe and then to the military road toward Fort Scott.

Colonel Jennison's troops were ordered out from their camps at the A.B.H. McGee Farm north of Westport, and Colonel Moonlight's troops marched from the Shawnee Indian Mission into place on Jennison's right, angling down in front of the state line south of Brush Creek. Moonlight's Eleventh was in position to either counter the Confederate left if it advanced or fall in behind Jennison and give support to the Federal right

Action along Brush Creek, October 23, 1864. *Courtesy of the Westport Historical Society.*

as it advanced. By this placement, Blunt could start the attack sooner and buy time for the Kansas militia units in Kansas City to move south in support of his advance—or retreat.

On the high ground south of Brush Creek, Colonel Shelby was preparing his attack. On the opposite bank, General Blunt, still stinging from Shelby's previous day's success, sent the Fourth Brigade under Colonel Ford and the First Brigade under Colonel Jennison surging forward through the icy waters, up the banks and onto the plateau south of Brush Creek. Stone fences enclosed the neat fields for miles around. A skirmish line was set up in a cornfield just south of the William Bent Home and west of Wornall's Lane. Shelby's Iron Brigade under M. Jeff Thompson was at the center of the Confederate forces advancing toward the Union position from about a mile away, just south of the Wornall Home. Units of Colonel Jackman's brigade were positioned on the flanks of Thompson's advance, while Fagan's brigades under Colonel Archibald S. Dobbin and Colonel W.F. Slemons were back in support of the line.

Out of the predawn mist came fire from the gray line. Answering quickly from Wornall's Lane came the fire from McClain's Independent Colorado Battery, followed by an increasingly steady fire from the Third Wisconsin Cavalry and the Fifteenth Kansas Cavalry as the figures in the distance became clearer. As the mist cleared, first light revealed that the gray lines had slowed. On the left, the attacking Confederates had gone to ground and started a steady fire into the Second Colorado Cavalry and the Sixteenth Kansas Cavalry. Over the course of the next hour, the pressure increased and steadily drove the Union line back down the hill and through the creek. Colonel Jennison's men retreated almost to the streets of Westport, while Colonel Moonlight's brigade was driven back across the Kansas border. It seemed as if the Confederates might win the battle at the start; however, Thompson was forced to pull up short. His troops were low on ammunition and were forced to hold at their position on the high ground on the south bank of Brush Creek. A chance for victory was lost in waiting, as Thompson was unable to press the advantage, and the Union line was able to recover.

General Curtis arrived at the Harris House Hotel and joined General Blunt on the roof as Blunt's forces were retreating back across Brush Creek. Curtis ordered Blunt to hold his advance until the Kansas militia troops being sent down from Kansas City were in place and then start his artillery barrage.

Waiting for an hour on the north side of Brush Creek, the Union cavalry troops watched as Blunt positioned his artillery and the militia units filed down from Kansas City. Then, all at once, the steady boom of cannon fire worked its way from the right side of the line to the ridge behind them, as projectiles were hurled into the trees and burst out of sight beyond the other side of the river. The Confederate batteries soon began to answer back. When Colonel Charles Blair arrived from Kansas City with reinforcements, the Union line readied once more to enter the icy waters of Brush Creek. Blair had brought his Third Brigade forward, along with the Ninth Wisconsin Battery and a section of artillery from the Colored Battery. Part of the Third Brigade joined the left of the Fourth, while the rest joined to the right of the Second Brigade. A battalion of the Twelfth Kansas State Militia arrived from Westport and joined with Colonel Moonlight's Second Brigade.

General Curtis joined Blunt along Brush Creek. Even though militia units were still coming down from Westport and Kansas City, Curtis decided to lead the advance himself. Taking the Ninth Wisconsin Battery and his escort, he prepared to order a general advance. Before the order could be given, Colonel Blair on the extreme right of the line, fearing he would soon be flanked, pushed across the river with the Fifth, Sixth and Tenth Kansas State Militia units. He sent a messenger to Curtis to inform him of his movement. Curtis sent the Nineteenth Kansas State Militia to support Blair, ordering it to swing in at his right. Blair's Third Brigade was now the Union extreme right, as General Blunt had sent Moonlight's Second Brigade to position itself between the Confederates and the Kansas line.

Curtis's escort included Company G of the Eleventh Kansas Cavalry and Lieutenant Edward Gill's two mountain howitzers, along with the Ninth Wisconsin Battery. Curtis ordered his troops forward and tried to attain the heights on the south bank with his cannons, only to be forced back again as Shelby reinforced his line.

Curtis regrouped on the north bank of Brush Creek once more and prepared for a third attempt at the high ground. As he began his advance, a Westport farmer approached General Curtis, offering to show him a narrow pass he could use to flank the Confederates. The farmer, named George Thoman, had had a pregnant mare stolen from him at gunpoint by men he believed were Confederates. Knowing they couldn't get far with the mare so close to foal, he set out to find it and ended up wandering into the Union lines. Thoman led Curtis to the gorge created by Swan Creek, a tiny tributary to Brush Creek, coming out just west and south of the Bent House. The Ninth Wisconsin quickly began firing down the line of Shelby's left flank. Shelby's men were caught by surprise, and his line began to waver and retreated from the crest. Captain Collins's four Parrott guns were wheeled into place, and Shelby's line re-formed as the artillery batteries engaged each other. Lieutenant Gill's mountain howitzers joined the Wisconsin battery in the duel.

While Curtis was at Swan Creek, Blunt had been pushing the third attempt up the south bank of Brush Creek with the First and Fourth Brigades. The Ninth Wisconsin's attack on the Rebel left spurred the Union rush on the heights. With a shout, they poured up and over into line along the stone fences Shelby's forces had abandoned under Curtis's fire. McClain's Colorado Battery's six rifled field pieces were placed in position on the crest on the west side of Wornall's Lane. Barker's five twelve-pounders joined in. Lieutenant D.C. Knowles's battery of the Second Kansas State Artillery and more pieces from militia units continued to add to the Union cannonade.

The Union center advanced, pushing Shelby's gray line back, but a charge by Colonel Slayback's Missourians restored it as the Union line moved back to the rock walls. Advancing again, the Union line was stopped by a flanking movement by Colonel Gordon's Fifth Missouri Confederate Cavalry.

For an hour, over forty cannons continuously fired. Collins's fire was so intense that it burst one of his Parrott guns. The blue line advanced steadily, taking over the lane south of the Bent House by noon. Shelby's brigades, along with Dobbin's brigade, had retreated to the line of stone walls just north of the Wornall Home.

More than thirty Federal cannons were tearing into the Rebel ranks. Collins had lost two more guns to Federal artillery fire and was down to his last Parrott. McClain's Colorado Battery had moved steadily forward along the west side of Wornall's Lane. As the guns were being repositioned, Colonel James H. McGehee's Confederate Arkansas Cavalry came up the lane, charging the guns. Colonel Jennison, on the right of the battery, realized that only quick action would save them. Quickly taking Company E of the Fifteenth Kansas Cavalry under Captain Curtis Johnson, he led a mad charge toward the left flank of McGehee's men. As the two cavalry units charged forward, a high-pitched yell came from McGehee's ranks. The two columns collided at an angle, and a tangle of horses and men descended into savage hand-to-hand combat. Captain Johnson and Colonel McGehee singled each other out as if by mutual consent for personal combat. Drawing their revolvers and charging each other, firing almost simultaneously, each hit his mark. Johnson took a bullet through his arm, and McGehee was shot in the chest. The mêlée, however, was turning in favor of the Confederates' greater numbers. Suddenly, two squadrons of the Second Colorado Cavalry that had been supporting McClain's battery charged into the Arkansans, who fled the field, leaving twenty-five dead and wounded and one hundred prisoners for the Federals on the field.

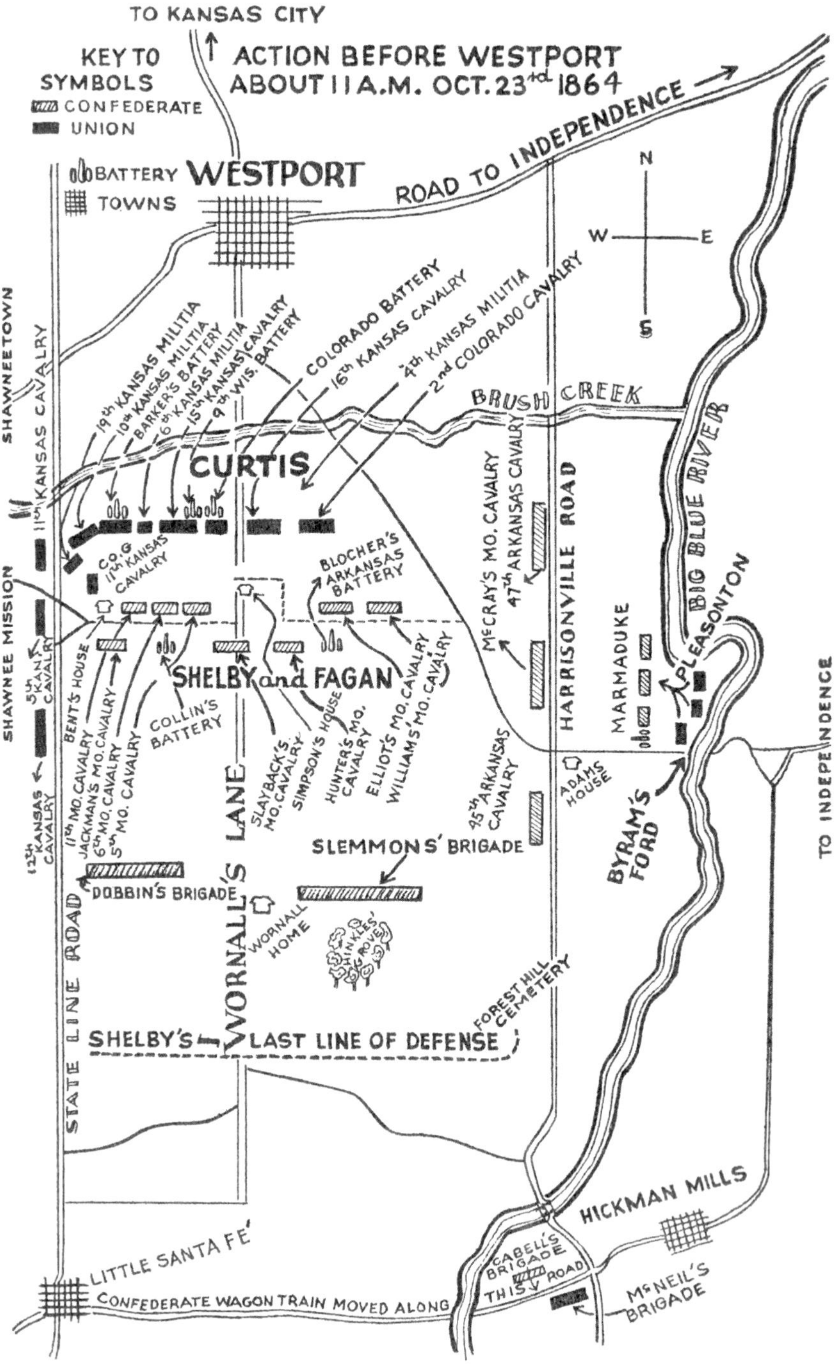

Map of the Battle of Westport showing the placement of troops about 11:00 a.m. on October 23, 1864. *Courtesy of the Westport Historical Society.*

Farther south on the Blue River, General Marmaduke's men had waited behind the captured Union defenses for Pleasonton's attack. General Rosecrans was still in Lexington on Saturday night and had ordered General A.J. Smith's infantry (which had finally come as near as Chapel Hill) to proceed toward Independence. Rosecrans left for Independence himself just after midnight. Pleasonton was sent orders to wait for Smith there as well. General Rosecrans wanted to concentrate his forces with Pleasonton's smaller cavalry force and Smith's infantry in order to have a force equal to Price's. (Reports of the size of Price's army were exaggerated.)

General A.J. Smith led infantry across the state in pursuit of Price and missed the Battle of Westport. *Courtesy of the Library of Congress.*

Pleasonton apparently did not receive the orders from Rosecrans and had been busy giving his own orders that night. He sent General John McNeil and the Second Brigade to Little Santa Fe to prevent Price's escape south and sent General Egbert Brown to Byram's Ford with orders to relieve Colonel Winslow's Fourth Brigade and attack at daybreak. (Third and Fourth Brigades were to support.) By sunrise, General Pleasonton was awake and listening for the sound of his advance. He continued for some time to wait in anticipation, but no booming cannon, no pop of small-arms fire, reached his ears. Mounting his horse and riding forward, he found General Brown still in consultation with Colonel Winslow while troops that he had ordered forward were sitting about camp. Pleasonton,

General Alfred Pleasonton organized the cavalry pursuit of Price from Jefferson City. *Courtesy of the Library of Congress.*

incensed by Brown's failure to implement orders, had General Brown arrested and placed Colonel John F. Phillips in command of the First Brigade with directions (along with Winslow's Fourth Brigade) to attack the Confederates at Byram's Ford immediately.

Colonel Winslow positioned Battery H of the Second Missouri Light artillery on a hill overlooking the road to the ford, with three three-inch Rodman guns. Under Lieutenant Phillip Smiley, the guns opened fire on the Rebel artillery and lead forces on the west bank of the river. Colonel Phillips dismounted his men and advanced toward the ford on the left side of the road, while Captain Dee and the Third Battalion of the Fourth Iowa Cavalry did the same through a wooded ravine three hundred yards to the right of the road. When Phillips's forces came into view, the west side of the river exploded with smoke and fire, pinning them down as artillery and sharpshooters poured lead into their ranks. Captain Dee managed to cross unnoticed by Marmaduke's pickets. Once

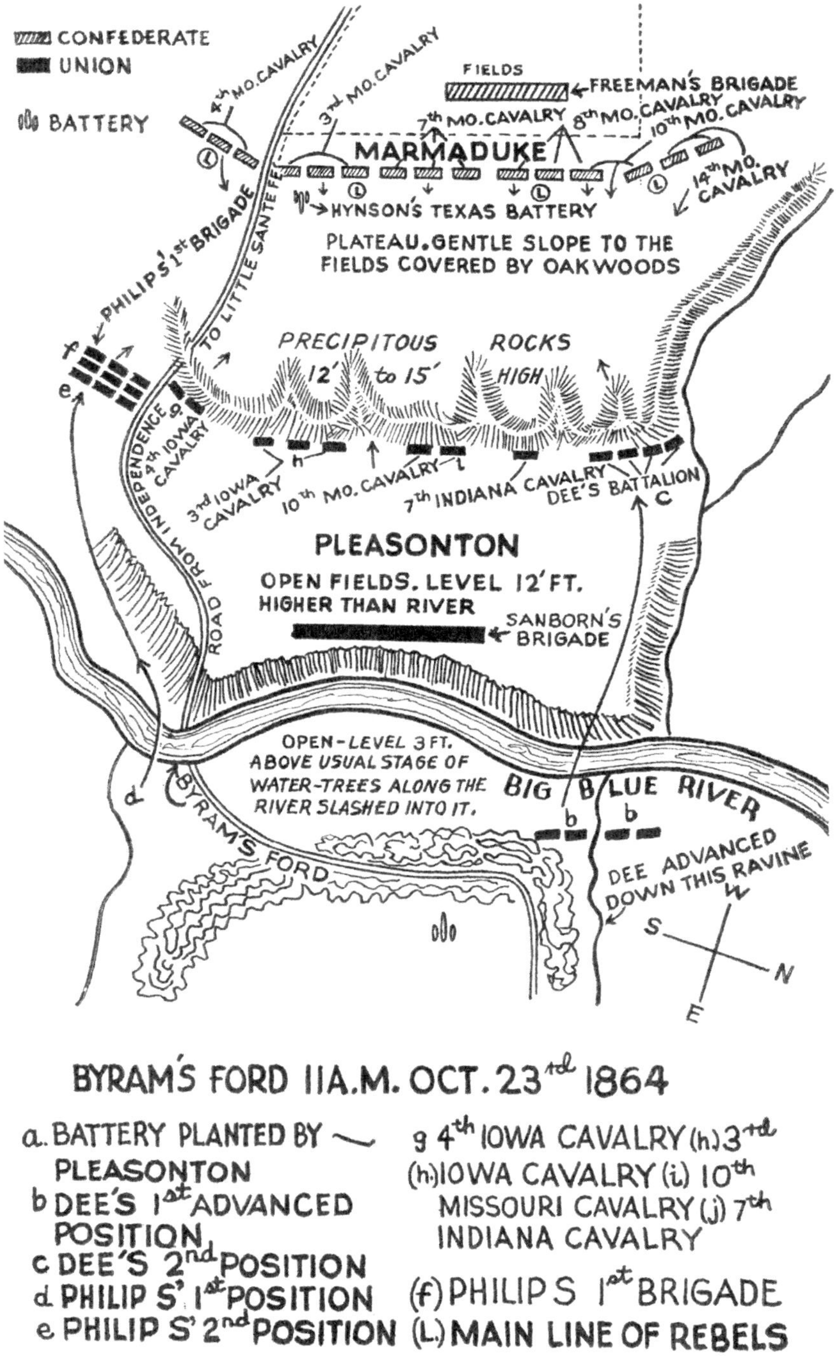

Map of the Battle at Byram's Ford showing the placement of troops at Byram's Ford by 11:00 a.m. on October 23, 1864. *Courtesy of the Westport Historical Society.*

they attained the west bank, the Iowans took to ground and began firing into the surprised Rebels' left. Phillips pressed forward into the river under terrific fire; many of his men were wounded or killed as they tried to cross the icy waters while holding rifles and ammunition boxes over their heads.

Once a foothold on the west bank had been established, the Confederate advance line retreated across a stretch of open ground that led to a long rock ledge, above which Marmaduke had placed his main line on a wooded hill that had two log houses near the crest serving as further cover for Rebel sharpshooters. Marmaduke had positioned Hynson's Texas Battery to cover the plain and the road.

Colonel Winslow led his Fourth Brigade across the river, riding their horses across, then dismounting and filling in the gap between Dee and Phillips's forces. Phillips's troopers mounted and pushed toward the rock ledge, but the horses could not scale the rocks there. The only avenue for cavalry to advance was the road, and then only in columns of four. Colonel Phillips sent the First Missouri State Militia Cavalry under Lieutenant Colonel B.F. Lazear up the road, only to be repulsed on both of two attempts. Lieutenant Colonel Thomas Theodore Crittenden led the Seventh Missouri State Militia Cavalry up the road, and one of his troopers returned to Colonel Phillips reporting that Crittenden had been killed. Phillips rode forward past the wounded and dead to find Crittenden alive but with the wind knocked out of him, having been hit in the chest by a spent bullet. All the units of the First and Fourth Brigades were involved in the fight by 11:00 a.m.

Probing forces found a cart path at the base of the rock ledge and pushed forward through it. The Fourth Iowa was the first of several dismounted groups of men to find a way over the ledge and forward. Colonel Winslow was wounded, so Lieutenant Colonel Frederick W. Benteen of the Tenth Missouri Cavalry took command of the Fourth Brigade. The advance topped the hill and drove Marmaduke's forces back into the woods and out into the fields. Pleasonton had suffered over two hundred casualties in gaining the heights. The Rodman guns were brought forward, and General Pleasonton, along with Sanborn's Third Brigade, joined Phillips and Dee. The Rodmans fired into the Confederate cavalry as it retreated. The First and Fourth Brigades re-formed as General Sanborn led the Third Brigade's pursuit of the Rebels toward the Harrisonville road.

Marmaduke's battered cavalry found some solace waiting at the Harrisonville road, as Fagan had moved there with Slemon's and McCray's brigades to help protect the Confederate right. Fagan had a section of Blocker's Arkansas Battery with him as well. Waiting for Marmaduke's men to pass through its lines, the battery opened on Sanborn's cavalry, stopping them long enough for Jackman (who had also been sent down the Harrisonville road by Shelby, albeit to protect the wagon train) to join forces with Fagan. Charging forward, Jackman and Fagan drove back Sanborn's right and pushed the brigade back across the Mockbee Farm in fierce hand-to-hand combat.

The desperate and sudden turn of events had pushed the Third to the breaking point, when Colonel Benteen, with the Tenth Missouri Union Cavalry, hit the Rebel flank hard, and the Rebels broke and ran. General

Twenty-pound Parrott guns. Heavy field artillery, the barrel alone weighed eighteen hundred pounds. *Courtesy of the Library of Congress.*

Pleasonton also came up at this point with the First Brigade. He sent Battery H forward to Hinkle's Grove, where they encountered Shelby's right flank. The gunners began firing into Shelby's Iron Brigade just as General Curtis ordered his general charge. Shelby's Iron Brigade was all that was left to oppose Curtis's advance. A blue line of cavalry advanced down Wornall's Lane, crashing into the Iron Brigade as another desperate and close fight began. Shelby and Thompson tried to rally their men, but a new line of fire belched out of Hinkle's Grove as Pleasonton's forces carved into the Iron Brigade's right flank. It was every man for himself at that point as Shelby's men threw away arms and equipment in a mad dash south. Stopping at a long line of stone fences, Shelby tried once more to re-form his lines.

Shelby would make one more stand. Fighting for time more than victory at this point, Shelby's troops held on stubbornly against the combined assault of Curtis and Pleasonton, buying Marmaduke and Fagan the chance to retreat down the state line with the wagon train and beef herd. Price's army was saved from complete disaster through their

William Bent–Seth Ward Home. Westport traders Bent and Ward lived successively in this home, which was used as cover by forces during the Battle of Westport. *Courtesy of the Jackson County Historical Society.*

efforts. Pleasonton's and Blunt's forces met on the state line and then continued to push south. They consulted with General Curtis and his staff at a farmhouse near Indian Creek, where the pursuit was tasked to Colonel Jennison's brigade and a battalion of the Second Colorado Cavalry. They continued the pursuit until dark, pressing the Rebels past Little Santa Fe toward the middle fork of the Grand River.

General John McNeil had been sent to Little Santa Fe and likely would have been in the way of the Rebel retreat had he moved more quickly toward it. McNeil had been sent south by Pleasonton to prevent the Rebel retreat, but he encountered General Cabell's men guarding the wagon train. Cabell set up a line of skirmishers, turning and firing on McNeil's Second Brigade and driving it back about a mile. McNeil tried to advance once, but the artillery duel that followed caused his troops again to fall back. McNeil remained in place until noon. Sterling Price, hearing the wagon train was in danger, came and put Tyler's unarmed recruits alongside the train to give the appearance that it was well guarded and pushed it into Little Santa Fe. McNeil tried again to advance, but Cabell's forces set fire to the prairie. The wind blew toward McNeil's men, and Cabell's troops fired round after round of Minié balls through the fire at them as well. McNeil had had enough. He remained out of the way but in sight while the wagon train, Marmaduke and the rest of the retreating Rebels headed down the military road to safety.

The road south was strewn with discarded equipment left by the withdrawing forces. The next morning, the pursuit would continue, and the next and the next.

The Morning After

There's always a morning after for those who survive a stirring or tragic event, a point when the moment of drama is past and one has a chance to take in the effect of the experience. On the morning of October 24, 1864, the great battle was done and the invader had been repelled and was being pursued by the victors. The people of Westport could breathe a moment and take it all in. It would be a later date before the full measure of the destruction could be absorbed, but on that Monday morning, it at least started to become clearer that the coming week's work would be the most daunting the town had ever faced (and perhaps ever would).

At the farms and homes nearest the battlefield, the impact had been immediate. The Wornall Home had been passed back and forth from army to army, riddled with bullets and filled with wounded and dying men from both sides. The destruction spread out from the homestead to the outbuildings and fields, where dead and wounded men and horses were scattered about like the fall leaves on the ground. Clothing, hats, swords, guns and all manner of equipment lay where they had fallen or been abandoned. The trees and vegetation were torn by the fire of cannons and thousands of bullets; the ground was trampled by horses, wagons and men. The unfortunate unknowns of the battle would soon be planted in the fields where they fought en masse with their brethren.

Nine-year-old Frank Wornall had stayed inside the home most of the day on Sunday, with the battle swirling around him. On Monday, his home had become a hospital and, to some degree, a morgue. The beautiful home was filled with the groans of wounded and dying men. More men waited outside the home, as there wasn't room for them all. Frank brought water and helped those he could. Outside, a pile of discarded parts from amputations was piling up nearly to the second story of the house. Near the barn, a pile of saddles from the dead horses found on the property numbered over one hundred.

The wagons went out from Westport as they always had, but this day they returned laden with men. The bumpy ride from field to town, over hills and across Brush Creek, would be made repeatedly throughout the day, as it had been made all through the day and night before. Homes and businesses quickly became hospitals, and just as so many of the men of Westport and Kansas City had suddenly become soldiers, the towns' women would abruptly become nurses. Mrs. Kersey Coates was

Lieutenant Colonel Thomas Theodore Crittenden was wounded at Byram's Ford. *Courtesy of the Library of Congress.*

seen hurrying down the street with fine curtains from her home, soon to become bandages. Mary C. Haverty had come to Westport a few years before and ran a select school for girls. The girls normally rode their horses to school, but after the battle, they rode as a group to the field to help the wounded of both sides. Women, regardless of which side they supported in the war, nursed soldiers, regardless of which side they had fought for. The suffering soldiers, so many of them young men and far from home, were the sole focus of their efforts. Father Donnelly would spend much of the next month ministering to the needs of the wounded in the city, and countless hours would be given freely by the women of the town.

The immediate challenge for those who remained behind was simply to scour the land for the dead and wounded and to sort them out. Identification of the dead and seriously injured was in some cases impossible. The ravages of bullets, cannon fire and horses' hooves, as well as a lack of uniforms or military identification, put the task out of reach. Men had been beheaded by cannon fire, and cavalry charges into artillery had left jumbled parts of men and horses in their wake. Families came to search the faces of the dead and the hospitals filled with wounded for loved ones or news of their fate. Some mass graves were dug and filled, as horses and men had to be buried quickly before putrefaction spread and with it disease. Many would be buried, dug up later, moved and reburied as families or friends learned of their whereabouts and disposition.

The medical corps had the daunting task of bringing order to the chaos. Wounded soldiers were often sick before they ever arrived at a field hospital. Pneumonia, dysentery and typhoid were the three most common killers. Diseases associated with childhood like measles or mumps were rampant in camps with young soldiers. Surgeons worked in non-sterile settings. The most common surgery was amputation; over thirty thousand amputations were performed by Union army surgeons during the course of the war, with a good surgeon only taking ten minutes to complete the operation. Despite the unsanitary conditions, nearly 75 percent of those who had an amputation survived. One of the more common types of ammunition used was the Minié ball, which was a high-caliber, slow-moving bullet that tended to shatter bone and force surgeons to amputate above the destroyed section of limb. Gut or head wounds tended to be fatal and often were put at the back of the line, behind amputations, which had a higher chance of success. Even if an amputation was successful, the threat of postsurgical infections like gangrene or pyemia (90 percent fatality rate) was constant, as the majority of surgeons lacked an adequate explanation for the cause of these diseases.

Pleasonton's surgeon in chief, Ferdinand V. Drayton, and Major Samuel B. Davis (division medical director of the Army of the Border) had the unenviable responsibility of coordinating the efforts of the various civilian and military medical personnel. The severely wounded from the twenty-second had been left in the field at Hickman Mills crossing, Byram's Ford and the state line. On the morning of October 23, Davis, along with Surgeon Phillip Harvey, had organized the regimental surgeons to form ambulance corps and had sent ambulances forward to pick up the wounded from the previous day's battle. But Sunday's fight had already

Union ambulance corps members practice the proper way to load the wounded into wagons. *Courtesy of the Library of Congress.*

begun, as many stranded wounded would learn from the sounds of battle as they lay where they had fallen and spent the night. Forced to wait until the awful battle ended, their challenge only became greater. The ambulance corps covered the battlefields from east of Independence to south of Hickman Mills. Severely wounded men were treated in the fields, being kept there until they died or were improved enough to be safely transported. Homes and businesses became field hospitals as wounded were gathered from the fields. The Wornall House became a field hospital mostly for the Confederate wounded. In Independence, a hospital was established under surgeon S.P. Earlickson. A temporary hospital was set up at Westport, where several members of the Second Regiment, Kansas State Militia, who had been wounded on the twenty-second were taken. Assistant Surgeon Graham took charge there.

There were larger hospitals set up at Westport, Independence and Kansas City, and a river steamboat (the *Tom Morgan*) even transported eighty-six of the wounded upriver to the Federal hospital at Fort Leavenworth, including those from Independence. Surgeon Harvey was placed in charge of all the field hospitals, as Surgeon Drayton had to rejoin Pleasonton and the pursuit.

Surgeon Drayton had very little time to waste. His army had moved on in pursuit of the Rebels, and he could not remain behind. Three days' provisions were sent to the field and general hospitals, and the dead were left to the citizens to deal with. The range of emotions experienced by the people of Westport during the following days must have been overwhelming.

As the sun rose on Sterling Price's Army of the Border, the wagons were put in line ready to continue the retreat. The troops were lined up in columns on both sides of the artillery and the undiminished wagon train, still protecting Price's loot. There was much grumbling about the wagon train, which once again would slow the army's retreat. "Old Pap" had led the Army of Missouri right into the Federal trap. At each creek or river crossing, the difficult task of marshaling the cattle and wagons across created a delay and a dangerous circumstance for the retreating men. Besides the dead comrades left behind, many of Price's men had been wounded and left in the field or on the side of the road, waiting to die or be taken prisoner. The wagons were a reminder, especially to the veteran troops, of the folly of the excursion, in which the preservation of the spoils had seemed to take precedence over that of the men.

The first hours of the morning had been lost in the process of trying to form the caravan into some semblance of order. The retreat had mixed units beyond recognition. Re-forming the brigades and gathering equipment and cattle, as well as civilian refugees, took precious time, as the Federal pursuit was sure to come sooner or later. As the hungry, fatigued remnants of Price's army continued their hard march south, a cold rain began to fall. The dreary weather accented the miserableness of their condition. There had been a drought in eastern Kansas that summer. The battered Confederates trudged past stunted and parched fields incapable of succor, while life-giving rain came only in time to mock their folly. Deserted farms, burned out by the border warfare, greeted them as they dogged along the lane. Some of the veteran troops had passed these same farms in 1861, when the fields were ripe and full and the homes were well tended and full of life. Now, blackened chimneys and beams presided over deserted piles of ash. The moist wind stirred and mixed the wood ashes with the smell of the teams, assaulting the senses from all quarters.

On the morning of the twenty-fourth, a pursuit column made up of General Pleasonton's provisional cavalry division and General Blunt's division of the Army of the Border set out from Little Santa Fe some twelve hours behind Price's retreating army. Colonel Moonlight, still with the Second Brigade, had shadowed Price's retreat on the Kansas side of the border in order to prevent Price from recrossing. Moonlight spent the night in Aubrey. Heading out about 10:00 a.m., the Union pursuit was pressed hard by General Curtis, who had assumed overall command. General Pleasonton had taken charge of the Missouri troops and Blunt the Kansans. Hungry and worn out from the constant riding and fighting, the Federal troops were likely in little better spirits than Price's men. General Curtis pushed them south after Price until 2:30 a.m.

The Long Retreat

The loss at Westport was but the beginning of the troubles the Army of Missouri would endure. "Old Pap" had marched them a thousand miles straight into a trap. Shelby had extricated his brigade and somehow managed to delay the Federal forces that threatened to engulf the survivors, but Price's damn wagon train had once again slowed the retreat. Half-starved, exhausted men who had alternated between fighting and marching for nearly a week started dropping out of the lines. Some just sat by the side of the road waiting to be captured.

It was about two thirty on Sunday afternoon when the various commanders of the Federal and state forces met to plan the pursuit of Price. General Curtis felt that a "vigorous pursuit" was necessary in order to protect the military posts and towns along the border from Price's forces. Governor Carney and General Deitzler wanted to disengage their troops and get them home in time to participate in the elections. General Pleasonton argued that his cavalry troops and horses were fatigued from the rapid pursuit across Missouri and the previous day's fight. Curtis decided to let Deitzler and members of the militia who lived north of Aubry muster out and return home, while Pleasonton and Blunt were ordered to pursue Price.

Monday morning, October 24, 1864, found Price's Army of the Border spread out in the disorganized heap into which they had fallen exhaustedly the night before. It took precious hours to gather and organize the cavalry, cattle, refugees and wagon train that sprawled from the middle fork of the Grand River to eight miles past Little Santa Fe. Price's army trudged across the state line into Kansas in two columns, with wagons and artillery in between. The preceding summer's drought, along with the cold rain that began to fall that afternoon, must have only intensified the dismal feelings and despair of the retreating Rebels.

The Federal pursuit had begun about ten o'clock in the morning on the twenty-fourth and continued until 2:30 a.m., stopping only briefly before taking up the pursuit before dawn on the twenty-fifth. Early that morning, Pleasonton's troops made contact with Price's rearguard pickets on the north bank of the Marais des Cygnes River. Driving forward, they soon found that Marmaduke's rearguard was spread out over several miles of open prairie between the Marais des Cygnes and Mine Creek. As Pleasonton pressed forward, Marmaduke's and General Fagan's divisions drew up into position for battle. Still crossing the creek and stretched

Disaster at Mine Creek, Kansas. A lopsided Union cavalry victory took place at Mine Creek. *Courtesy of the Westport Historical Society.*

out for miles beyond was General Price's wagon train. Union artillery began targeting the wagons, while Rebel artillery on the left fired into Pleasonton's First Brigade, led by Colonel Phillips. Lieutenant Colonel Frederick Benteen with the Fourth Brigade joined Colonel Phillips, and the two brigades charged the Rebel left and center.

The mêlée that followed drove the Confederates back into the churning waters of Mine Creek as artillery ripped through the floundering men, cattle and wagons in the creek. Wagons loaded with ammunition caught fire, adding the explosion of cartridges and shells to the noise and confusion. T.R. Freeman's brigade of Marmaduke's division left the field altogether, leaving behind a large gap in the Confederate line into which Union troops poured. Seizing the Rebel artillery, the Union troops turned it, firing into the retreating Confederates. A few minutes later, Generals Cabell and Marmaduke were captured, along with over five

General John S. Marmaduke, captured at the Battle of Mine Creek, later became Missouri governor. *Courtesy of the Library of Congress.*

hundred of their men. The Federal attack at Mine Creek sent many of Price's remaining troops running south in a panic, dropping weapons and gear as they fled.

General Price left his ambulance and rode back to Mine Creek to assess the situation. General Shelby was sent toward Fort Scott to see if it could be captured, but Price sent word for him to return. Shelby raced back, but the rout at Mine Creek had sent Confederate troops reeling in confusion. Shelby formed a line on a low ridge about a mile south of the Little Osage River. All he could do at this point was delay the Federal advance. General John McNeil's brigade relieved Colonel Phillips's brigade and, along with Colonel Benteen, continued to press the Rebel line. With a series of cavalry maneuvers, Shelby was able to delay the advance of Pleasonton once again, with the help of M. Jeff Thompson and the Iron Brigade, but only for about an hour. The encroaching Federals threatened both flanks and forced Shelby to withdraw, leaving Colonel Sidney Jackman to cover the retreat. Shelby took up a new position just north of the Marmaton, while Jackman charged the Federals. The Confederates were able to hold the new position until nightfall. Price gathered and burned nearly a third of his wagons the next morning (October 26), leaving early and moving much faster.

Once again, Curtis had an opportunity to destroy Price's command, and once again circumstances prevented it. General Pleasonton had followed Price to the point where he felt that Fort Scott was safe, as Price's train had taken the fork away from the fort. Badly in need of rest and rations, Pleasonton took Phillips's and Sanborn's brigades toward Fort Scott. General Blunt, assuming that Pleasonton had been ordered there, followed suit. General Curtis, seeing Pleasonton leave the pursuit, rode after him, and an argument between the generals ensued. Both men were major generals, and though Curtis was in command, Pleasonton was also under the command of General Rosecrans, who outranked Curtis. Pleasonton sent a message from Fort Scott to General Rosecrans suggesting that the pursuit of Price, at least for the Missouri troops, should end. Then he notified Curtis that due to poor health he could no longer continue the chase.

The remaining Federal troops continued to follow Price's army, stopping at 3:00 a.m. on the twenty-seventh at the ruins of Carthage, Missouri, to rest and eat. Resuming the pursuit with General Blunt taking the lead, the Federals again caught up with the Rebel army at Newtonia, Missouri. Blunt had only two of his brigades with him when he approached Newtonia about 2:00 p.m. on the twenty-eighth. The rest of the Federal army had stopped to eat and feed their horses.

Blunt attacked, but again Shelby defended and with a larger force. Blunt used McClain's Colorado Battery and Patterson's Mountain Howitzers to soften the Rebel line. The Sixteenth Kansas Cavalry and the Second Colorado Cavalry were sent plunging into Shelby's force, but the line held. Blunt sent the rest of his force into the battle. Shelby probed the Union right but was repulsed. As the fighting became more intense, Shelby sent troops through a cornfield to attempt to flank the Federal left. Blunt was outnumbered and began to pull back. General Sanborn arrived at that time and sent dismounted troops into the cornfield, turning the Rebel right and ending the battle as Shelby withdrew into the night.

General Curtis had closed again on Price and might have destroyed his army the next day, but fate again intervened. General Rosecrans sent orders on October 29 recalling the Missouri troops, reducing Curtis's force to about twenty-five hundred men. Curtis, angered and disappointed by the turn of events, wired General Halleck in Washington, laying the failure of the pursuit of Price's army at Rosecrans's feet. Halleck wired back to Curtis orders from General Grant to continue the pursuit with the Missouri forces down to the Arkansas River. Unfortunately, the orders came too late to do any real good. Sanborn, Phillips and McNeil were either too far away or unwilling to rapidly respond to an order that countermanded the orders of their immediate superior. Benteen came to join Curtis but didn't arrive at Neosho to join the pursuit until November 1. Curtis managed to chase off some troops of Price's that had detached to attack the Federal garrison at Fayetteville, but most of the remnants of Price's army had escaped.

Price's remaining forces crossed the Arkansas River on November 7, just thirty miles west of Fort Smith. General Curtis sent his pursuing army home. After Price crossed the Arkansas, he furloughed Cabell's and Slemons's brigades. The rest of his troops followed him into Indian Territory, crossing through Choctaw land and finally into Texas. Hunger to the point of starvation, along with smallpox, plagued the army. By November 23, they reached Bonham, Texas. Turning east, they dragged into Laynesport, Arkansas, on December 2, 1864.

The Aftermath

The Union had won. The failure of Price at Westport foreshadowed the failure of the Confederacy, in spite of its last-ditch and desperate plans. Lincoln was reelected. The war, what was left of it, would be fought in the South. The West would open up to the railroad, the telegraph and the plow.

Missouri would continue to be a seat of rebellion. In 1866, ten thousand Federal troops would be sent there to enforce order. The battle had ended, but the fight wasn't over. Reverend Thomas Johnson would be murdered at his home on January 2, 1865. The motive for the murder was likely Johnson's agreeing to swear an oath of allegiance to the U.S. government (Johnson owned slaves and might have been seen as a turncoat). In the West, there would be no more grand battles, but assassinations and reprisals continued in attempts to settle old scores. Some of the guerrillas who survived (like Frank and Jesse James) would resist Federal authority and lash out at representatives of eastern influence, banks and railroads for years to come. Generals Price and Shelby had fought on to the bitter end and beyond, taking the remnants of Price's army into Mexico. They stopped only to bury their battle flag in the Rio Grande rather than surrender it or themselves to the enemy.

Many in Westport would suffer under Reconstruction. Those with Southern backgrounds or who had supported the rebellion would be ostracized under the new Missouri constitution. By and large, however, Missourians would get back to the business of life.

Colonel Kersey Coates led the Kansas City Home Guard during the Battle of Westport. *Courtesy of the Jackson County Historical Society.*

Westport, freed of the constant threat of war, began again to prosper, but the city that had grown up along the riverfront was quickly surpassing it. Kansas City (through the actions of Van Horn, Coates and Charles E. Kearney) would finally have a railroad bridge built to connect it to the major lines coming from the East. It would become a central shipping point for the grain and cattle raised in the nearby hinterland. The meatpacking industry, among others, would help build a metropolis on the plains near the banks of the Missouri and Kaw Rivers.

After the war, Missouri drafted a new constitution, but in order to remain in control, the radical Republicans placed a number of restrictions on nearly anyone who supported the South. A test oath of loyalty became a requirement not only for office, but it was also administered to voters in order to exercise the franchise. Anyone who had supported the Confederacy, even if he had not acted on his beliefs, was banned from public office, from voting and even from becoming a member of the clergy.

Returning Missourians who had fought for the Confederacy and former guerrillas were treated nearly the same. Harassed, marginalized and maltreated by the occupying forces as well as local authorities, they were often treated with suspicion or contempt by those who had supported the Union. Many ended up leaving the state. Men like Cole Younger and Frank James found little incentive to make peace with the new regime. Former aide to General Shelby, John N. Edwards became editor of the *Kansas City Times* and chronicled the misfortunes that followed the former Rebels. Edwards published a book, *Notable Guerrillas*, glamorizing the ex-Rebels and likening the James brothers to Robin Hood. Edwards would publish letters, purportedly from Jesse James, either proclaiming his innocence of accused crimes or justifying his actions against the railroads and banks as retribution for their unjust actions against Missouri's poor. Stories, both real and imagined, spread of the James brothers' generosity to widows of former Confederates and to poor working folk. Taking great risks, robbing the wealthy banks and railroads and escaping or outgunning larger forces were all part of the legend that grew beyond the men involved.

As part of the "Lost Cause" movement, Southern authors began rewriting the South's part in the war. Placing states' rights above slavery as the primary reason for secession, former Confederate supporters attempted to justify and explain their tragic role. As the country had been forced back together, it was the South's burden to supply a narrative that could console the living, honor the dead and reconcile the past with the new order.

For sympathetic eyes, there was genuine injury and injustice to which the ex-Rebels could point. The harsh Reconstruction-era constitution and test oath were scrapped (the oath being declared unconstitutional by the U.S. Supreme Court). The Democratic Party regained control of Jackson County and has held a clear majority here ever since.

The "outlaw as Robin Hood" characterization lived on in hundreds of popular dime novels and western magazines and was perpetuated in the movies. Nearly forty years after Jesse James's death, Jesse James Jr. would play his father in the first of dozens of movies that have been made about the outlaw gang in the last century. Emmett Dalton, bank robber and cousin to the Younger brothers, would play himself in a movie after serving a prison sentence, as did (female outlaw Belle Starr's nephew) Henry Starr, who was killed while robbing another bank two years after playing himself in the movie *A Debtor to the Law*.

Missouri's Harry Truman, though he was born twenty years after the Battle of Westport, would be affected greatly by the generations that had experienced the Civil War firsthand. His mother, Martha Ellen Young-Truman, was the daughter of Solomon Young, a prosperous slave-owning farmer. During the Civil War, Kansas raiders known as "Red Legs" under Senator James Lane, after forcing Martha's mother Hariette Young to serve them lunch, looted her family home, taking personal possessions, including the family silverware. They also took or killed the livestock, including one hundred hogs they couldn't take with them. Martha's sister, Sarah Young, was married to ex-guerrilla Jim Chiles. Truman's uncle by marriage, Jim was killed in a shootout on the Independence Square with Deputy City Marshal James Peacock. Harry Truman was named after Martha's brother, Harrison Young, who was tortured by Kansas Red Legs in an attempt to get him to become an informant against Missourians loyal to the South. Harrison Young refused to become an informant even after being repeatedly hanged and then let down by the Red Legs. One of Martha's other brothers, William Young, served with Confederate colonel Upton Hayes. Truman's grandmother Hariette Young was forced out of her home and put in a prison camp under Order Number 11. Truman grew up hearing firsthand accounts of the wrongs suffered on the Missouri side of the border and developed sympathy for those who seemed to have been forced into the roles they had by circumstances beyond their control. He is quoted: "But Quantrill and his men were no more bandits than the men on the other side. I've been to reunions of Quantrill's men two or three times. All they were trying to do was protect the property on the Missouri side of the line."

The impact of the Battle of Westport could scarcely be seen up close. In the short term, Price gained little and expended a great deal of effort to get it. By drawing more Federal troops into Missouri, he probably strengthened the Union's grip on the state. The loss at Westport did little to help the Confederacy's recruiting efforts in Missouri. Price had to burn part of his wagon train and lost more men than he gained in recruits, so the shortage of men and supplies remained constant. The raid probably

Senator Harry Truman with Vice President Garner looking at guns once owned by Jesse James. *Courtesy of the Library of Congress.*

didn't have any effect at all on the duration of the Civil War, and the election results were as expected, despite the South's attempts to interfere.

It is in the lives of those who witnessed, fought and survived the great battle that the effects stretch forth through the generations since. Many politicians of nineteenth-century Kansas and Missouri directly experienced the conflict leading up to and including the Battle of Westport. Citizens of the burned district in the border counties who grew up in the late nineteenth and early twentieth centuries, like Harry Truman, learned of the era through the words of those who lived it.

The list of participants in the Battle of Westport who went on to fame or infamy, or who had already achieved positions of note, is quite exceptional. A partial list includes:

General Sterling Price had already served as a brigadier general of volunteers in the Mexican-American War, a representative in both the Missouri and United States Houses of Representatives and as governor and bank commissioner for the State of Missouri. Price owned slaves and had a tobacco plantation, but he started the war opposed to secession. His attempt after the war to keep his army intact and enter the service of Maximilian of Mexico ultimately failed, and he returned to Missouri. Financially ruined and with his health failing, he died in St. Louis on September 29, 1867. The funeral was one of the largest the town had known.

GENERAL JO SHELBY would also return to Missouri after the fall of Maximilian in 1867. He involved himself in various business activities but refused to run for office. Shelby served as a character witness in the trial of Frank James (James was acquitted) and supported Confederate veterans' organizations. In 1893, Shelby was appointed a federal marshal for the Western District of Missouri. He was endorsed for the position by former governor of Missouri Thomas Fletcher (who had fought against Shelby during the war) and ex–commander in chief of the Grand Army of the Republic William Warner. Fletcher spoke to President Grover Cleveland about the appointment, assuring him that it was Shelby who had most influenced ex-Confederates in Missouri to accept the new order and that Shelby's influence with Missourians was "inestimable." Though many Northern newspapers opposed the appointment, letters from veterans from both armies came to Shelby's defense, and the appointment went through. The next year, Shelby helped to preserve order in his district during the Pullman Strike, overseeing a force of over seven hundred special deputies. He remained in office until his death on February 13, 1897, and his funeral, like Price's, was one of the largest the town had seen. His monument stands in a prominent position in Union Cemetery.

GENERAL WILLIAM S. ROSECRANS served as minister to Mexico briefly after the war and became involved in a number of speculative ventures with mixed success. He was elected to Congress as a representative from California. He also served as register of the treasury from 1885 to 1893. He died on March 11, 1898.

GENERAL JOHN S. MARMADUKE came from a long line of successful politicians; his father was Meredith Miles Marmaduke (eighth governor of Missouri) and his great-grandfather was John Breathitt, governor of Kentucky, who died in office. After the war, Marmaduke ran for the office of governor and lost to former Union general Thomas Crittenden in 1880.

Four years later, Marmaduke won the governorship, but like his great-grandfather, he would die in office (of pneumonia on December 28, 1887).

General Samuel R. Curtis was mayor of Keokuk, Iowa, and served two and a half terms as a member of the U.S. House of Representatives prior to the Civil War. After the war, he served as a railroad commissioner. He died on December 26, 1866.

General Alfred Pleasonton continued to serve in the army after the war. He left the service in 1868 and began work as a collector of internal revenue. He was then appointed commissioner of internal revenue under Ulysses S. Grant. He was president of the Terre Haute and Cincinnati Railroad for a short time. He died on February 17, 1897. The towns of Pleasanton, Kansas, and Pleasanton, California, were named after him; both misspelled his name.

Colonel Thomas Moonlight entered politics after the Civil War, serving as Kansas secretary of state, Kansas state senator, adjutant general of the state of Kansas, governor of the Wyoming Territory and finally as U.S. minister to Bolivia. He died on February 7, 1899, and is buried at Muncie Cemetery in Fort Leavenworth, Kansas.

Colonel Charles Jennison served two terms in the Kansas House of Representatives and one in the state senate. He died on June 21, 1884.

General John Sanborn served one term in the Minnesota House of Representatives and one in its senate before the war and once more in each after the war. He served on the Indian Peace Commission after having negotiated several treaties, along with William Bent and Kit Carson. Sanborn also helped negotiate the Medicine Lodge Treaty. He was elected president of the Minnesota Historical Society in 1903 and died a year later on May 6, 1904.

James Butler Hickok served as a scout and spy for General John Sanborn, riding with Price's forces for most of the raid, separating off sometime after the Battle of Westport. Hickok's exploits as scout, deputy to the provost marshal at Springfield and marshal in various western towns became legendary. Stories about Hickok's exploits appeared in *Harper's Weekly* and in a number of dime novels. Hickok worked for a while for his old friend William Cody, touring with a program called "Scouts of the Plains." But by 1876, Hickok had joined the latest gold rush in South Dakota, ending up dead in Deadwood, shot in the back of the head while playing poker on August 2, 1876. Hickok's fame continued long after his death, as his story was told and retold in western novels, comic books and even on television. He was also portrayed in over a dozen movies stretching from 1923 to the present.

WILLIAM FREDERICK "BUFFALO BILL" CODY lived in Leavenworth, Kansas, and went to work at age eleven after the death of his abolitionist father from injuries he'd received in a confrontation with pro-slavery men. Cody worked as a "boy extra" for Alexander Majors's freighting firm and a few years later was a Pony Express rider for him as well. In 1863, Cody joined Company H of the Seventh Kansas Cavalry. He went on to fame and fortune after the Battle of Westport. After the war, he served as an army scout, and in 1872 he was awarded the Medal of Honor. He toured with "Wild Bill" Hickok and "Texas Jack" Omohundro in a program called

William "Buffalo Bill" Cody worked for Alexander Majors and fought under Colonel Jennison at the Battle of Westport. *Courtesy of the Library of Congress.*

"Scouts of the Plains." In 1883, he found lasting success with the creation of his Wild West show. Cody put together ensemble casts of frontier scouts, Indians, trick riders, trick shots, etc. The show glamorized the image many people in the eastern states (and in Europe) would have of the American West. The town of Cody, Wyoming, was founded by him and named after him. The Cody Dam on the Shoshone River was named after him posthumously for his work in promoting irrigation and its building. Cody was depicted in dime novels, western magazines and movies. He played himself in two early silent films. He died on January 10, 1917.

Lieutenant Colonel Preston Plumb was elected to the Kansas House of Representatives in 1862 and then joined the Eleventh Kansas Cavalry later that year. He returned to the House of Representatives and became the Speaker in 1868. He was elected to represent Kansas in the United States Senate in 1877. He served as chairman of the Committee on Public Lands and was reelected twice. He died in office during his third term as senator on December 20, 1891.

John "Liver Eating" Johnson was a mountain man and trapper on whom the fictional character Jeremiah Johnson was based. Johnson was a member of Company H, Second Colorado Cavalry. He was wounded in action (gunshot to the shoulder) on the morning of October 23 (probably in fighting around Loose Park). He died on January 21, 1900.

Colonel John F. Phillips served as mayor of Sedalia and commissioner of the Missouri Supreme Court (1883–85). He served as judge of the Kansas City Court of Appeals (1885–88) and was appointed U.S. judge of the Western District of Missouri by President Grover Cleveland. He died on March 13, 1919.

Colonel James Fleming Fagan was not paroled by the U.S. government until June 1865, after which he returned to farming in Arkansas. Fagan's stepfather, Samuel Adams, was governor of Arkansas. Fagan had served in the U.S. Army, achieving the rank of lieutenant during the Mexican-American War. In 1875, despite his service in the Confederacy, General Grant appointed Fagan U.S. marshal. In 1877, he served as receiver in the U.S. Land Office. Fagan died on September 1, 1893.

Colonel William Lewis Cabell was one of seven brothers who served in the Confederate army. Cabell graduated from the United States Military Academy in 1850, served in the U.S. Army until the outbreak of the Civil War and then joined the Confederacy. After the war, he returned to Fort Smith, Arkansas, and worked as a civil engineer until he passed the bar and began practicing law. He moved to Dallas, Texas, in 1872 and was elected mayor in 1874. He served a total of four terms as mayor. Cabell was appointed U.S. marshal in Fort Worth, serving from 1885 until 1889. He supported Confederate veterans' groups, helping to secure pensions, establish veterans' homes and build cemeteries. Cabell was commander of the Trans-Mississippi Department of the United Confederate Veterans. He died on February 21, 1911.

LIEUTENANT COLONEL FREDERICK WILLIAM BENTEEN continued to serve in the army until he retired in 1888. He is best known for his actions (or for choosing not to act on Custer's orders) at the Battle of Little Bighorn in Montana rather than his role at Westport and Mine Creek.

COLONEL JOHN MCNEIL served in the Missouri legislature in 1844. After his service in the war, he was clerk of the criminal court in St. Louis County, then county sheriff, then clerk of the criminal court again, then commissioner to the Centennial Exposition in Philadelphia, then inspector for the U.S. Indian Service and finally superintendent of the St. Louis branch of the U.S. Post Office.

JOHNNY RINGO was known for his connection to the Earp-Clanton feud that erupted in Tombstone, Arizona, at the O.K. Corral in 1881. John H. Monnett, in his introduction to the revised edition of *Action before Westport, 1864*, asserts that his father (Howard N. Monnett) found evidence that places Ringo with Jo Shelby on Price's 1864 raid. Ringo lived in Liberty and Gallatin, Missouri. He knew Frank and Jesse James and was a cousin to the Youngers.

JIM CHILES was uncle to Harry S Truman and a member of Quantrill's guerrillas. He served with Shelby early in the war and then later with Quantrill. He ended up back with Shelby by the time he went to Mexico, likely joining during Price's raid. Jim returned to Missouri after the war and found his land foreclosed and his opportunities greatly diminished as a former Rebel. He was killed in a shootout on the Independence Square with city marshal James Peacock. Harry grew up knowing his Chiles cousins and his aunt, Sarah Young-Chiles, and hearing tales of the Missouri guerrillas. He even attended a few of the reunions that Quantrill's men had in Independence.

Colonel Samuel J. Crawford served in the Kansas legislature and was the third governor of Kansas. He served on General Curtis's staff at Westport and Mine Creek. He was elected in November 1864 and then reelected in the subsequent election. He died on October 21, 1913.

Colonel John L. Beveridge of the Seventeenth Illinois Cavalry became sheriff of Cook County, then a state senator, a congressman from Illinois, lieutenant governor, governor of Illinois and finally assistant United States treasurer.

Colonel Sidney D. Jackman became a rancher after the war. He served as a representative in the Texas legislature and was appointed U.S. marshal for western Texas by Grover Cleveland. He died on June 2, 1886.

Colonel Thomas T. Crittenden became governor of Missouri but was demonized for offering bounty on Jesse James and others "dead or alive" without benefit of trial for their alleged crimes.

General Thomas Ewing Jr. was the first chief justice of Kansas. After the war, he was a two-term congressman from Ohio. He had higher aspirations, but Order Number 11 hounded his career.

Appendix

Organization of Troops in the Battle of Westport

Organization of the Army of Missouri (Confederate)

Major General Sterling Price, Commander
Major William W. Dunlap, Chief of Artillery

Division Commanders

Major General James F. Fagan
Major General John S. Marmaduke
Brigadier General Joseph O. Shelby

Fagan's Division
Brigadier William L. Cabell
Colonel Archibald S. Dobbin
Colonel William F. Slemons
Colonel Thomas H. McCray

Cabell's Brigade
Gordon's Arkansas Cavalry, Colonel Anderson Gordon
Gunter's Arkansas Cavalry Battalion, Lieutenant Colonel Thomas M. Gunter
Harrell's Arkansas Cavalry Battalion, Lieutenant Colonel John M. Harrell

Hill's Arkansas Cavalry, Major J.L. Adams
Monroe's Arkansas Cavalry, Colonel James C. Monroe
Morgan's Arkansas Cavalry, Colonel Thomas J. Morgan
Witherspoon's Arkansas Cavalry Battalion, Major J.L. Witherspoon
Hughey's Arkansas Battery (two guns), Captain William M. Hughey

Dobbin's Brigade
Dobbin's Arkansas Cavalry, Colonel Archibald S. Dobbin
McGehee's Arkansas Cavalry, Colonel James H. McGehee (wounded October 23) and Lieutenant Colonel Jesse S. Grider
Witt's Arkansas Cavalry, Colonel A.R. Witt
Blocher's Arkansas Battery (two guns), Lieutenant J.V. Zimmerman

Slemons's Brigade
2nd Arkansas Cavalry, Colonel William F. Slemons
Carlton's Arkansas Cavalry, Colonel Charles H. Carlton (wounded October 22) and Lieutenant Colonel R.H. Thompson
Crawford's Arkansas Cavalry, Colonel William A. Crawford
Wright's Arkansas Cavalry, Colonel John C. Wright
Stirman's Arkansas Cavalry Battalion, Lieutenant Colonel Ras Stirman

McCray's Brigade
50th Missouri Cavalry, Colonel Timothy Reeves
45th Arkansas Infantry (mounted), Colonel Milton D. Baber (captured October 22)
47th Arkansas Infantry (mounted), Colonel Lee Crandall

Unattached
Anderson's Arkansas Cavalry Battalion, Captain William L. Anderson
Lyle's Arkansas Cavalry, Colonel Oliver P. Lyle
Rogan's Arkansas Cavalry, Colonel James W. Rogan

MARMADUKE'S DIVISION
Brigadier General John B. Clark Jr.
Colonel Thomas R. Freeman
Major Joseph H. Pratt (Artillery)

Clark's Brigade

Escort: Company D, 5th Missouri Cavalry

3rd Missouri Cavalry, Colonel Colton Greene (wounded October 21) and Captain Benjamin S. Johnson (October 23)

4th Missouri Cavalry, Colonel John Q. Burbridge (wounded October 21) and Lieutenant Colonel William J. Preston

7th Missouri Cavalry, Colonel Solomon G. Kitchen (wounded October 23)

8th Missouri Cavalry, Colonel William L. Jeffers

10th Missouri Cavalry, Colonel Robert R. Lawther

14th Missouri Cavalry Battalion, Lieutenant Colonel Robert C. Wood

Davies's Missouri Cavalry Battalion, Lieutenant Colonel J.F. Davies

Hogane's Engineer Company, Captain James T. Hogane

Freeman's Brigade

Ford's Arkansas Cavalry Battalion, Lieutenant Colonel Barney Ford

Freeman's Missouri Cavalry, Lieutenant Colonel Joseph R. Love (taken prisoner October 23) and Major William Cook

Fristoe's Missouri Cavalry, Colonel Edward T. Fristoe

Pratt's Artillery

Harris's Missouri Battery (three guns), Lieutenant T.J. Williams

Hynson's Texas Battery (three guns), Captain Henry C. Hynson

Shelby's Division

Brigadier General M. Jeff Thompson (Shelby's Iron Brigade)

Colonel Sidney D. Jackman

Colonel Charles H. Tyler

Shelby's Iron Brigade (Thompson's Brigade)

5th Missouri Cavalry, Colonel Frank B. Gordon

11th Missouri Cavalry, Colonel Moses W. Smith

12th Missouri Cavalry, Lieutenant Colonel William H. Erwin

Elliott's Missouri Cavalry, Colonel Benjamin F. Elliott

Johnson's Cavalry Battalion, Major Rector Johnson

Slayback's Missouri Cavalry Battalion, Lieutenant Colonel Alonzo Slayback

Collins's Missouri Battery (two Parrott guns), Captain Richard A. Collins

Jackman's Brigade
Crisp's Cavalry Battalion, Lieutenant Colonel John T. Crisp
Hunter's Missouri Cavalry, Colonel DeWitt C. Hunter
Jackman's Missouri Cavalry, Lieutenant Colonel C.H. Nichols
Schnable's Missouri Cavalry Battalion, Lieutenant Colonel John A. Schnable
Williams's Missouri Cavalry Battalion, Lieutenant Colonel D.A. Williams
Connor's Missouri Battery (two Parrott guns), Lieutenant Jacob D. Connor

Tyler's Brigade
Coffee's Missouri Cavalry, Colonel J.T. Coffee
Perkins's Missouri Cavalry, Colonel Caleb Perkins
Searcey's Missouri Cavalry, Colonel James T. Searcey
Unorganized recruits

Unattached
46th Arkansas Infantry (mounted), Colonel W.O. Coleman

ORGANIZATION OF THE ARMY OF THE BORDER (UNION)

Major General Samuel R. Curtis, Commander

DEPARTMENT OF KANSAS

Escort: Company G, 11th Kansas Cavalry, Captain G.L. Gove
Two-Gun Battery, Lieutenant Edward Gill

DIVISION COMMANDERS

Major General James G. Blunt
Major General George W. Dietzler

Blunt's Provisional Cavalry Division
Colonel Charles R. Jennison
Colonel Thomas Moonlight
Colonel Charles W. Blair
Colonel James H. Ford

Jennison's First Brigade, 15th Kansas Cavalry
3rd Wisconsin Cavalry (Detachment), Captain Robert Carpenter
15th Kansas Cavalry, Lieutenant Colonel George H. Hoyt
Foster's Missouri Cavalry Battalion, Captain George S. Grover
Battery (five guns) manned by 15th Kansas Cavalry, Lieutenant Henry L. Barker

Moonlight's Second Brigade, 11th Kansas Cavalry
5th Kansas Cavalry (Companies L and M), Captain James H. Young
11th Kansas Cavalry, Lieutenant Colonel Preston B. Plumb
16th Kansas Cavalry (Companies A and D), Lieutenant Colonel Samuel Walker
Battery (four guns) manned by Company E, 11th Kansas Cavalry

Blair's Third Brigade, 14th Kansas Cavalry
4th Kansas Militia, Colonel W.D. McCain
5th Kansas Militia, Colonel G.A. Colton
6th Kansas Militia, Colonel James D. Snoddy (arrested October 16) and Colonel James Montgomery
10th Kansas Militia, Colonel William Pennock
14th Kansas Cavalry (Company E), Lieutenant William B. Clark
19th Kansas Militia, Colonel A.C. Hogan
24th Kansas Militia Battalion, Lieutenant Colonel George Eaves
2nd Kansas State Artillery (two guns), Lieutenant Daniel C. Knowles
9th Wisconsin Battery (four guns), Captain James H. Dodge

Ford's Fourth Brigade, Second Colorado Cavalry
2nd Colorado Cavalry, Major J. Nelson Smith (killed October 21) and Major J.H. Pritchard

16th Kansas Cavalry (Detachment), Major James Ketner

McLain's Independent Colorado Battery (six rifled field guns), Captain W.D. McLain

Kansas State Militia Division

Major General Dietzler
Brigadier General M.S. Grant
Brigadier General William H.M. Fishback

Units (Not Brigaded)

1st Kansas Militia, Colonel Charles H. Robinson

2nd Kansas Militia, Colonel George W. Veale

2nd Kansas Colored Militia, Captain James L. Rafferty and Captain Richard J. Hinton

3rd Kansas Militia, Colonel Charles Willemsen

7th Kansas Militia, Colonel Peter McFarland

9th Kansas Militia, Colonel Frank M. Tracy

12th Kansas Militia, Colonel L.S. Treat

13th Kansas Militia, Colonel Alexander S. Johnson

14th Kansas Militia, Colonel William Gordon

18th Kansas Militia, Colonel Matthew Quigg

20th Kansas Militia, Colonel J.B. Hubbell

21st Kansas Militia, Colonel Sandy Lowe

22nd Kansas Militia, Colonel William Weer

Artillery

Independent Colored Battery (two guns), Lieutenant Patrick H. Minor

Leavenworth Battery, Kansas Militia Light Artillery (two guns), Captain Gustavus Zesch (assumed command October 20)

Topeka Battery of 2nd Kansas Militia (one gun), Captain Joseph Cracklin

Grover's Battery of 3rd Kansas Militia (two guns), Captain Joel Grover

Unattached Unit

Kansas City Home Guards, Colonel Kersey Coates

Organization of the Army of the Department of Missouri

Major General William S. Rosecrans, Commander
Major General Alfred S. Pleasonton, Division Commander, Provisional Cavalry Division

Brigade commanders

Brigadier General Egbert B. Brown (arrested October 23)
Colonel John F. Phillips, 7th Missouri Militia Cavalry
Brigadier General John McNeil
Brigadier General John b. Sanborn
Colonel Edward F. Winslow, 4th Iowa Cavalry (wounded October 23)
Lieutenant Colonel Frederick W. Benteen, 10th Missouri Cavalry

Brown's (then Phillips's) First Brigade
1st Iowa Cavalry (Detachment), Major John McDermott
1st Missouri Militia Cavalry, Colonel James McFerran (arrested October 23) and Lieutenant Colonel Bazel Lazear
4th Missouri Militia Cavalry, Major George W. Kelly
7th Missouri Militia Cavalry, Colonel John F. Phillips and Lieutenant Colonel Thomas T. Crittenden

McNeil's Second Brigade
2nd Missouri Cavalry (Detachment), Captain George M. Houston
3rd Missouri Militia Cavalry (Detachment), Lieutenant Colonelo Henry M. Mathews
5th Missouri Militia Cavalry, Lieutenant Colonel Joseph Eppstein
7th Kansas Cavalry, Major Francis Malone
9th Missouri Militia Cavalry (Detachment), Lieutenant Colonel Daniel M. Draper
13th Missouri Cavalry, Colonel Edwin C. Catherwood
17th Illinois Cavalry, Colonel John C. Beveridge

SANBORN'S THIRD BRIGADE
2nd Arkansas Cavalry, Colonel John F. Phelps
6th Missouri Militia Cavalry (Detachment), Major William Plumb
6th Enrolled Missouri Militia Cavalry (Detachment), Lieutenant Colonel John F. McMahan
7th Enrolled Missouri Militia Cavalry (Detachment), Major W.B. Mitchell
8th Missouri Militia Cavalry, Colonel Joseph J. Gravely

WINSLOW'S (THEN BENTEEN'S) FOURTH BRIGADE
3rd Iowa Cavalry, Major Benjamin S. Jones
4th Iowa Cavalry, Major Abial R. Pierce
4th Missouri Cavalry (Detachment), Captain George D. Knispel
7th Indiana Cavalry (Detachment), Major S.W. Simonson
10th Missouri Cavalry, Lieutenant Colonel Frederick W. Benteen and then Major William H. Lusk

COLONEL NELSON COLE'S 2ND MISSOURI LIGHT ARTILLERY
Company H, 2nd Missouri Light Artillery (two guns), Captain William C.F. Montgomery and Lieutenant Philip Smiley
Company L, 2nd Missouri Light Artillery (four guns), Captain Charles H. Thurber
Battery (two guns) of 5th Missouri Militia Cavalry, Lieutenant Adam Hillerich

UNASSIGNED
2nd New Jersey Cavalry (Detachment), Captain Michael Gallagher
19th Pennsylvania Cavalry (Detachment)

Organization of the 16th Army Corp (A Detachment of the 1st and 3rd Divisions)

Major General A.J. Smith, Commander

Division Commanders

Colonel Joseph J. Woods
Colonel David Moore

Woods's First Division
Colonel Lucius F. Hubbard, 5th Minnesota Infantry
Colonel Sylvester G. Hill, 35th Iowa Infantry

Hubbard's Second Brigade
5th Minnesota Infantry
7th Minnesota Infantry
8th Wisconsin Infantry
9th Minnesota Infantry
10th Minnesota Infantry
12th Iowa Infantry
47th Illinois Infantry
Battery G, 2nd Illinois Light Artillery (six guns)

Hill's Third Brigade
33rd Missouri Infantry
35th Iowa Infantry

Moore's Third Division
Colonel T. J. Kinney, 119th Illinois Infantry
Colonel James I. Gilbert, 27th Iowa Infantry
Colonel Edward H. Wolfe, 52nd Indiana Infantry

Kinney's First Brigade
58th Illinois Infantry
89th Indiana Infantry
119th Illinois Infantry

Gilbert's Second Brigade
14th Iowa Infantry
24th Missouri Infantry

27th Iowa Infantry
32nd Iowa Infantry

Wolfe's Third Brigade
49th Illinois Infantry
52nd Indiana Infantry
117th Illinois Infantry
178th New York Infantry
3rd Indiana Battery (four guns)
9th Indiana Battery (four guns)

Bibliography

Barnes, Jeff. *Forts of the Northern Plains*. Mechanicsburg, PA: Stackpole Books, 2008.

Barton, O.S., with notes by Albert Castel and commentary by Herman Hattaway. *Three Years with Quantrill: A True Story Told by His Scout John McCorkle.* Norman: University of Oklahoma Press, 1992.

Big Blue Union [Marysville, Kansas], November 5, 1864.

Brown, A. Theodore. *Frontier Community: Kansas City to 1870.* Columbia: University of Missouri Press, 1963.

Brown, A. Theodore, and Lyle W. Dorsett. *K.C.: A History of Kansas City, Missouri.* Boulder, CO: Pruett Publishing Co., 1978.

Brownlee, Richard S. *Gray Ghosts of the Confederacy: Guerrilla Warfare in the West, 1961–1865.* Baton Rouge: Louisiana State University Press, 1958, 1986.

Castel, Albert. *A Frontier State at War: Kansas 1861–1865.* Lawrence, KS: Heritage Press for the American Historical Society, 1958. New material by Edward E. Leslie, 1992.

———. *General Sterling Price and the Civil War in the West.* Baton Rouge: Louisiana State University Press, 1968.

Davis, Dale E. "Guerrilla Operations in the Civil War: Assessing Compound Warfare During Price's Raid." Master's thesis, U.S. Army Command and General Staff College, Fort Leavenworth, KS, 2004.

DeAngelo, Dory. *Voices Across Time.* Kansas City, MO: Tapestry Publications, 1987.

Denny, James, and John Bradbury. *The Civil War's First Blood: Missouri 1854–1861.* Boonville: Missouri Life Inc., 2007.

Edwards, John N. *Noted Guerrillas, or The Warfare of the Border: Being a History of the Lives and Adventures of Quantrill, Bill Anderson, George Todd, David Poole,*

Fletcher Taylor, Peyton Long, Oll Shepherd, Arch Clements, John Maupin, Tuck and Woot Hill, Wm. Gregg, Thomas Maupin, the James Brothers, the Younger Brothers, Arthur McCoy and Numerous Other Well-Known Guerrillas of the West. St. Louis, MO: Bryan Brand, 1887.

Faragher, John Mack. *Daniel Boone: The Life and Legend of an American Pioneer.* New York: Henry Holt & Co., 1992.

Gilmore, Donald L. *Civil War on the Missouri-Kansas Border.* Gretna, LA: Pelican Publishing Co. Inc., 2006.

Goff, William A. *Old Westport.* Westport, MO: Westport Historical Society, 1977.

Goodrich, Thomas. *Guerrilla Warfare on the Western Border, 1861–1865: Black Flag.* Bloomington: Indiana University Press, 1995.

Hill, Robert (Mrs.). "War Letter from Independence [to Mrs. Kate Doneghy]," *Kansas City Genealogist* 31, no. 4 (Spring 1991): 182–83.

Hinton, Richard J. *Rebel Invasion of Missouri and Kansas and the Campaign of the Army of the Border against General Sterling Price, in October and November, 1864.* Chicago: Church, Goodman and Connelley, 1865.

The Independent [Oskaloosa, Kansas], October 29, 1864.

Jackson, David W., and Paul Kirkman. *Lockdown: Outlaws, Lawmen and Frontier Justice in Jackson County, Missouri.* Independence, MO: Jackson County Historical Society, 2009.

Lee, Fred L. *Gettysburg of the West: The Battle of Westport, October 21–23, 1864.* Kansas City, MO: Westport Historical Society, 1976.

Liberty Tribune [Liberty, Missouri], October 28, 1864; and November 4, 1864.

Monaghan, Jay. *Civil War on the Western Border, 1854–1865.* New York: Bonanza Books, 1955.

Monnett, Howard N. *Action Before Westport 1864.* Revised ed. Boulder: University Press of Colorado, 1995.

New York Daily Tribune, October 24, 1864.

Smokey Hill and Republican Union [Junction City, Kansas], October 29, 1864.

Steele, Philip W., and Steve Cotrell. *Civil War in the Ozarks.* Gretna, LA: Pelican Publishing, 1993.

United States War Department. *The War of the Rebellion: A Compilation of the Official Records of the Union and Confederate Armies.* Vol. 41. Washington, D.C.: Government Printing Office, 1880–1901.

Webb, W.L. *Battles and Biographies of Missourians*. Kansas City, MO: Hudson-Kimberly Publishing, 1900.

Westport Historical Society. *Site-Seeing in Old Westport.* Westport, MO, 1995.

White Cloud Kansas Chief [White Cloud, Kansas], October 27, 1864.

Whitney, Carrie Westlake. *Kansas City Missouri: Its History and Its People, 1808–1908.* Chicago: S.J. Clarke Publishing Co., 1908.

Zeinert, Karen. *Tragic Prelude Bleeding Kansas.* North Haven, CT: Linnett Books, 2001.

Index

K

L

M

N

O

P

U

V

W

Y

About the Author

Paul Kirkman is an author, historian and speaker who lives in Independence, Missouri, with his wife, Shawn, and daughter, Shannon. Paul has his BA in history from Columbia College and has worked as an archival assistant in the Archives of the Kansas City Department of Parks, Recreation & Boulevards and as a speaker for the State Historical Society of Missouri Speakers' Bureau. Paul coauthored *Lockdown: Outlaws, Lawmen & Frontier Justice in Jackson County, Missouri* with archivist David W. Jackson of the Jackson County, Missouri Historical Society.